The 27 Club

Why Age 27 Is Important

Published in 2012 and 2018 (revised) by
Kahurangi Press, Tauranga, New Zealand
www.kahurangi-press.com
Copyright © 2018 Michael Owen

A CIP (Cataloguing-in-Publication) record for this book is
available from National Library of New Zealand
ISBN 978-0-473-20684-0

Book design and typography: Michael Owen
Copy editor: Angela Rockel

Cover: Icarus (unknown artist)

Also by Michael Owen (available from Amazon)
Jung and the Native American Moon Cycles, 2002
The Maya Book of Life: Understanding the Xultun Tarot, 2011
All the Rough Beasts: The Death of the Earth, Part 1, 2018

www.deathoftheearth.com
www.xultun.com
www.kahurangi-press.com

THE 27 CLUB

Why Age 27 Is Important

Michael Owen

Kahurangi Press

For T

and the bird
and the 17s

CONTENTS

Preface

> Great talents are the most lovely and often the most
> dangerous fruits on the tree of humanity. They hang
> upon the most slender twigs that are easily snapped
> off. —C G Jung

What is the 27 Club? It is the collective's term for a group of
famous rock stars such as Jimi Hendrix, Janis Joplin, Kurt
Cobain, and Amy Winehouse, all of whom died at the age
of 27. The 27 Club does not exist, some say. It's a journalis-
tic convenience, a meme, a stereotype that is not supported
by the scientific evidence. True. But a stereotype is only the
social face of an underlying archetype. The notion of the
27 Club, stripped of the artificial precision of age, points to
something that does exist.

First, what this book is not. It is not an attempt to prove
or disprove the existence of the 27 Club. That I will leave
to the fevered debunkers and rationalists, enslaved by their
left hemispheres, who go to great lengths to prove it's an irrational myth. (And, yes, those two words are often put in
the same sentence.)

The death of a rock star at age 27 is too literal and bind-
ing a notion for something that is one of the great patterns
in our lives—this time in our late twenties when, for specific developmental reasons, we have an opportunity for
more life or more death. So let's defocus a bit and abandon the notion of a specific age and the constrictions of a
number. That gives the precisionists and statisticians too
much leeway and we become blinded to an experience that
is defined not by age and number but by psychology and
circumstance.

Second, what this book is. It is about a style of consciousness and living which can lead to stories of both tragedy and beauty around age 27 but which is actually spread throughout the twenties. It was characterised by the Swiss psychiatrist, C G Jung as puer[1] or puella consciousness (Latin for girl or boy, young man or young woman).

The puer is the archetype of the eternal youth, the often brilliant and creative person who remains younger than his or her age, soars high, and crashes and burns. It is not bound by age but rather by personality; there are puers in their sixties or seventies. But if the phenomenon is not age-dependent—if there are adolescent pensioners—why does popular culture focus on age 27 and the 27 Club? It's because normal psychological forces bring us to a crossroads in our late twenties. This is not as widely recognised a stage as, say, infancy (0–3), preschool (3–6), childhood (6–12) or adolescence (12–18). Psychology, for the most part, does not have much to say about emotional and spiritual development after 18. But we continue to grow and change even after we become an adult, physically and cognitively.

I shall use an indigenous teaching called the Moon Cycles to give a more nuanced understanding of what happens in our late twenties.[2] The Moon Cycles have nothing to do with astrology or numerology. They are about an archetypal pattern of time as measured by the feminine cycles of the moon instead of the masculine movements of the sun.

I will not go into depth about the highly visible lives of rock stars like Jimi Hendrix and Jim Morrison who have

---

[1] For convenience, I shall use the term puer throughout to apply to both men and women.

[2] For an in-depth look at the Moon Cycles see Michael Owen, *Jung and the Native American Moon Cycles: Rhythms of Influence*,

become the founding members of the 27 Club—the famous few who get all the attention. That has been done already and it's easy to cherry-pick their lyrics to confirm your theories. But not much has been written about all the accountants, computer programmers or plumbers who have died at 27.

In an interview on USA National Public Radio in 2009, Eric Segalstad said that age 27 was around the time when people go from youth to maturity and that people who died at that age were not all victims of rock 'n' roll stardom. Some died in accidents and murders. Others didn't live hard, like Pete Ham of Badfinger, victim of dishonest managers and record label fights that left him penniless.[3] The circumstances, method and particulars of an individual's death are not my concern here. Rather, it is the question, "Did they live out the archetype of the eternal youth?"

It is not a matter of "believing" or "disbelieving" in the existence of the 27 Club. Much too black and white. Belief, disbelief, faith, conviction and principles offer an escape hatch when we run into paradox, complexity, ambivalence, absurdity, chaos and contradiction. Belief, with its left-hand of gullibility and superstition, and its right-hand of rationality and scepticism (yes, superstition and rationality are two sides of the same coin) drains everything of colour and depth. It flattens, it simplifies, and makes us simpletons. So I invite the reader to temporarily suspend belief or disbelief and any principles or convictions that might divert you into one or the other. The ultimate test of something is whether or not it works in the human soul. I will leave the reader to decide if the patterns sketched this book have meaning for them, or not.

---

[3] "Before I Get Old: 'The 27s' Made Early Exits: NPR." www.npr.org/2009/04/05/102670912/before-i-get-old-the-27s-made-early-exits

Because this book is about the early deaths of those in the 27 Club and other Clubs it has many stories of tragedy and suicide. There is another story of equal importance about success and joy in life. But that's another book.

But I do **caution** the reader who may be vulnerable to thoughts of hero worship or admiration for the 27 Club. Or those who harbour thoughts of self-harm or suicide which may intensify when you read this book. If in doubt, put the book down. Suicide is never just suicide. It's complicated. And it's often suicide *at* someone (including yourself). So do what works for you to keep breathing. That's all you have to do. Just this next breath. It will pass. That way you get to see how your story unfolds.

Chapter 1 explores the psychology of the eternal youth and how this psychology helps us understand those in the 27 Club. Chapters 2, 3 and 4 look at the patterns of the Big Moon Cycles and the Chaotic Journeys which help us answer the question, "Why age 27?" Chapter 5 on The Little Moons describes in more detail the Big South Moon from birth to age 27. Chapter 6 summarises the little that science has to say about the 27 Club and development in our 20s.

Volumes have already been written about the lives of 27 Club members. Another one is not needed. This is not a definitive study but rather a rough, initial sketch, so you will not find extensive referencing but I have given the occasional footnote. I am indebted to the Twisted Hairs and Harley SwiftDeer Reagan for the teachings of the Moon Cycles. and to the writings of C. G. Jung, Marie-Louise von Franz and James Hillman.

—Michael Owen
Maenam, August 2018

1

Puer

Only the good die young. —Billy Joel

Don't trust anyone over thirty. —Jerry Rubin

Better to burn out than fade away.
                    —Neil Young, *Rust Never Sleeps*

Hope I die before I get old.
                    —The Who, *My Generation*

I wanna live fast, die young and leave a beautiful corpse. —Pretty Boy Romano[4]

The young Greek gods who died and were reborn, such as Iacchus, Dionysus, Attis, Narcissus, Icarus, Phaeton, Adonis and Eros, were all called by the name puer. They were gods of life, death and resurrection. There were fewer puella goddesses; Artemis is an example. The moon and

---

[4] In a 1949 movie *Knock on Any Door* with Humphrey Bogart, Pretty Boy Romano, a young hoodlum accused of murder, said, "I wanna live fast..." Often attributed to James Dean.

the feminine die and are reborn every month and have less need for the drama.

Puer

The puer looks like a young girl and the puella looks like a young boy. He or she could go either way. He is the archetype of change itself whereby the old dies and is born anew. Steve Jobs said, "Death is very likely the single best invention of Life. It is Life's change agent. It clears out the old to make way for the new." That's a puer statement.

Like all archetypes, the puer is bi-polar and two-faced with a "positive" and a "negative" face. The positive side of the puer appears as the Divine Child who symbolises newness, potential for growth, and hope for the future. The negative side is the child-man who refuses to grow up and meet the challenges of life head on, waiting instead for his ship—or a woman—to come in and make everything right. Peter Pans are always on the lookout for Wendys.

The mark of a puer is not the age of death (although the great majority of those in the 27 Club and surrounding Clubs are puers) but an archetypal style of consciousness and personality at any age. Perhaps you know one, have been one, are one. The older a person gets though, the greater the tension between their chronological age and their psychological age. If this tension becomes too great, something has to give, and the result is an accident, a depression, an overdose, a relationship, or death.

In modern times, the puer is Michael Jackson who lived in Neverland and had pyjama parties with young boys. He is Peter Pan, the magic boy who is pitted against the evil Captain Hook, a "grown-up."

The puer is James Dean, famous for his role as the troubled, disaffected young man in *Rebel Without a Cause*. The director, Elia Kazan, said of Dean, "He was nuts, he was a psychopath. He was crazy, near-sighted, always having trouble with women. He was very talented, very sensitive, very clinging. There were gaping wounds in him." Dean died in a car crash when he was 24.[5]

He is Timothy Treadwell (April 29, 1957 – October 5, 2003, 46 years 5 months 6 days). After surviving alcoholism and a near-fatal heroin overdose in the late 1980s Treadwell styled himself an amateur expert on grizzlies and believed that his mission was to protect bears. He was criticised for his lack of basic safety precautions in his interactions with the coastal grizzly bears of Katmai National Park, Alaska among whom he lived for 13 summers. At the end of the 13th summer he and his girlfriend Amie Huguenard were killed and eaten by a grizzly. He was the subject of the 2005 film "Grizzly Man" by Werner Herzog.[6]

He is Steve Irwin (February 22, 1962 – September 4, 2006, 44 years 6 months 13 days), an Australian TV personality and wildlife expert known as "The Crocodile Hunter." He was killed by a stingray while filming underwater.

Psychologically, the term puer/puella applies to men and women who remain adolescent into their adult years. They never really grow up unlike most of us who have to grow up willingly or unwillingly, sooner or later. They resist growing up, selling out, becoming part of the herd, the rat-race, the hated "society." As the years progress the tension between their chronological age and their psychological

---

[5] As quoted by Mary Blume, International Herald Tribune, December 13–14, 1969.
[6] Sally Porterfield, Keith Polette and Tita Baumlin. *Perpetual adolescence: Jungian analyses of American media, literature, and pop culture.* SUNY Press, 2009

age becomes unsustainable and, like a rubber band that's been stretched too far, their life snaps. Relationship messes, break-downs of some sort, or death, is the result. Sentimental eulogies are given about how he packed so much living into his few years, how brightly he burned, but never about the death and self-destruction that everyone knew would happen sooner or later.

Marie-Louise von Franz said that with the puer there is "a kind of asocial individualism: being something special, one has no need to adapt, for that would be impossible for such a hidden genius, and so on. In addition, an arrogant attitude arises toward other people, due to both an inferiority complex and false feelings of superiority… with the secret thought that one day one will be able to save the world; the last word in philosophy, or religion, or politics, or art, or something else, will be found."

But, she goes on, the one thing dreaded by the puer is "being pinned down, of entering space and time completely, and of being the singular human being that one is…. At the same time, there is a highly symbolic fascination for dangerous sports—particularly flying and mountaineering—so as to get as high as possible, the symbolism being to get away from reality, from the earth, from ordinary life. If this type of complex is very pronounced, many such men die young in airplane crashes and mountaineering accidents."[7]

Robert Bly describes the puer as follows: "These flying people, giddily spiritual, do not inhabit their own bodies well, and are open to terrible shocks of abandonment. They are averse to boredom. Among the fliers are most ashram habitués; devotees of higher consciousness determined to

---

[7] Marie-Louise von Franz, *The Problem of the Puer Aeternus,* 3rd ed. Toronto: Inner City Books. p. 8.

avoid earthly food; platonic lovers, celibates, and Don Juans, ready to leave each one when they fail to find the missing pearl.... Some say that a man's task in the first half of his life is to become bonded to matter: to learn a craft."[8]

So, on the light side, the puer is creative, daring, risk-taking, idealistic, and imaginative. On the dark side, the puer hates to grow old, is always seeking, and pines for his youth. He tends to be untidy, disliking too much order, exhibitionistic, forgetful of responsibilities, never turns up on time, and likes distractions and escapes. He is often dangerous but attractive to women, he never wants to be tied down, is always preparing to say goodbye and leave, hates rules and responsibilities, is bitter about being a misunderstood genius, hates routine, always has great ideas that are about to hatch, dislikes hard work (except hard work he likes) and is often drawn to spiritual pursuits. Common puer dreams are those of imprisonment—chains, bars, cages, bondage. Life is experienced as a prison.

Innocence

The puer tends to be a believer, and is easily impressed, naive and idealistic. He is afflicted by honesty and openness. So he will attract his shadow—con-men, deceivers, and all manner of devious and dubious people. He may be attracted to a spiritual group but is blind to the shadowy aspects of the leader or guru. In close relationships he is too much of the "good boy" and may attract or be attracted

---

[8] Robert Bly, *A Gathering of Men*. Audio. Mystic Fire Video, 1989.

to an overbearing partner. He may be "pussy-whipped" or unable to defend himself from attack.

Outwardly, he is limp and accommodating but his shadow is cruel, cold and unfeeling. He may show great charm and be interesting and attractive, physically, intellectually and spiritually, but emotionally he has a feeling function that does not work very well.

He may surprise his partner by his sudden coldness and if things get too much he may leave abruptly. But just as he writes relationships off quickly he will also write himself off quickly, leading in the extreme to suicide. He has little attachment, relatedness, intimacy, or bonding to the other. He may coldly plan the death of the relationship (by affair, by leaving, by cruelty, or even by murder) or his own death. He wants to be something or someone else at some time, but he does not want to be the actual human being he is, now. The archetype that he is living is the dying god and he has a nostalgic longing for death. The one who is possessed by the puer must die, either psychologically—in which case the death is followed by a rebirth—or physically, in which case it's permanent.

The puer longs and yearns. His eyes become misty on hearing the anthem or the pledge of allegiance. He melts at the thought of the soul-mate and once-in-a-lifetime love. He reaches with a hand, like Michelangelo's David, palm facing upward just so, for the high, ethereal notes of the unattainable, the ungraspable, and the incomprehensible. He is always searching for the awe of the great mystery that is beyond human grasp.

There is another kind of puer though, a negative puer you might say, who is the same on the inside but looks different on the outside. And they often live side-by-side in the same person. He is the introverted puer who is sleepy, dozy and lazy. He's a slacker, no raw wilderness for him, no vigorous exercise, no health food and fasting, no hair-shirt meditation retreats, no wild flights of creativity. He loves his suburban comforts, his couch, his dope and his video games. His imagination can just reach to the heights of channel-surfing. He sinks into whatever warm place is at hand. He may be on the benefit, the dole, or welfare, and is terminally work-shy. He's Beavis and Butthead. One type of puer sinks into the swamp, the other escapes into the sky.

The warrior, nature boy and couch surfer are all versions of the puer. All are driven to heroically exceed themselves—as is right and proper around 18 to 24. But this stage has an expiry date and begins to smell by the late twenties. The heroic excess of many rock star members of the 27 Club was not death on the battlefield or the cliff face; they were not eaten by a grizzly, nor did they die of lethargy and over-slacking. They died from a heroin overdose. Heroin (dia-cetylmorphine) was first synthesised by the chemist Felix Hoffman of the Bayer company in 1897. He tested it on some of Bayer's workers who said it made them feel "he-roic" (heroisch) or "strong" and so coined the name.

Nature boy

Actaeon, a young hunter wandering in the woods, chanced upon Artemis the moon-goddess, also known as the Lady of the Beasts, bathing naked in the forest. As punishment for seeing her nakedness, Artemis turned him into a stag. He was then torn apart by his own hunting dogs. Artemis also sent a scorpion to kill the young Orion after he acci-dentally touched her.

Actaeon is the young boy's desire to know, to explore the wonder of nature. Artemis is the purity of nature, of unpolluted streams, unconquered peaks, the remote forest, the undiscovered Shangri-La, the unseen waterfall. But Artemis is also the death-bringer aspect of pure nature, with no concern for human feeling—the cliff does not weep for the falling climber, the surf does not hear the drowning swimmer.

Artemis was the elder twin of Apollo, the sun god, and her mother Leto laboured 9 days and 9 nights to give birth. The delivery of Artemis was painless but the birth of Apollo lasted for nine days and nights because jealous Hera had kidnapped Eileithyia, the goddess of childbirth, to prevent Leto from having an easy and painless labour. With the absence of Eileithyia, Artemis was the one who helped her mother deliver her twin brother, Apollo. Artemis is the moonlight and splendour of the night but her dark side is Hecate, the goddess of sorcery and witchcraft, who represents the darkness and terrors of the night. On moonless nights Hecate roamed the earth with a pack of ghostly, howling dogs. Her ancient gift, beyond even the power of Zeus to deny, was to bestow or withhold from mortals any desired gift.

People since the time before time have gone to the forest and the mountains to find what is hidden in themselves. It is in nature that our own nature reveals itself. Artemis doesn't live in the city. Artemis is virginal. She is not contaminated by the trappings of culture. She is the psyche that has a mind of its own uncoloured by thoughts, attitudes and expectations that come from the world outside. She is the psyche that does not foist its psychology onto others and the world around it, forcing them to carry what the individual is unconscious of.

In ancient Greece, Artemis was the goddess, not of childbirth, but of mothering and the young. She is not maternal in the usual way but she governs the care of what is not yet formed or mature. In ancient Greece, young girls, at age 9, were consecrated to Artemis. So anything in a culture or an individual that is new, developing, not yet ripe, not ready to show to the world, on virgin soil, exploring new territory, filled with the spirit of adventure, wanting to take flight, doing just for the sake of doing, is under the care of Artemis.

The puer does not want careful thought or thinking through, or working it out, having a goal or a structure. He wants to be a free spirit, moving from town to town, less government, less taxes, the Wild West, no picket fence and family for him, imagination and freedom is all.

So Actaeon wanders. He is not on a journey heading somewhere, he does not have a map, or a goal. He wanders as the impulse takes him. But he wanders into something that is too big for him. Actaeon, in his puer innocence, does not have the wisdom, experience, street-smarts, bush-lore, commonsense or sage advice needed to go walkies in the bush at night. He is unprepared for a confrontation with nature itself and pays with his life. He is betrayed by those animals he thought most loyal to him, his dogs. His boyish innocence is in fact murderous. In New Zealand, tourists die every year, innocent of the power of the bush and the sea. They lose their way in the denseness of the bush, in heavy rain, and die of hypothermia. Or fall down cliffs. Or drown in rips.

In the last week of April 2003 Aron Ralston was hiking in the Canyonlands National Park, Utah. A suspended boulder from which he was climbing down became dislodged, crushing his right forearm and pinning it against the canyon wall. On the sixth day he amputated his own forearm and was eventually rescued. In 1997 Ralston had begun the goal of climbing all 53 of Colorado's "fourteen-ers" or peaks over 14,000 feet high, solo and during win-ter—a feat that had never been achieved. He subsequently reached his goal in 2005. His story has been made into a movie, *127 Hours*—a heroic story much idealised—but we should note Ralston's puer act of hubris in the face of nature. He never notified anyone of his planned route. The amputation took place when Ralston was 27 years 6 months and 4 days old.

So it is with those who, uninitiated, play on the edge—surfing, climbing, sky diving, base jumping. Staring death down, but without the right spiritual equipment, so to speak. The outdoor puer is drawn to extreme sports like a moth to a flame. The indoor puer is drawn to extreme causes. He buys derivatives, currency speculates, or joins PETA. The puer, and his shadow side-kick the warrior, wants to die with his boots on, riding the big wave, crash-ing and burning in a blaze of glory. They get all sentimen-tally suicidal about life being over, throw themselves from the windows if the stock market collapses, if they can't do big deals, have as much sex/drugs/money as they want, if they can't save the world, prosecute the corporate pol-luters, surf the big ones, or ski the back mountains. They can't bear for their bodies and the physical world to not be forever young.

The daring, imagination, idealism, creativity and phys-ical athleticism associated with the puer can easily slide into an obsession with self-sufficiency, and further into a narcissistic haze of arrogance, pride, righteousness and purity. Now the puer thinks he is beyond the human ken and plays recklessly with dangerous borders. We read about it every Sunday morning. Saturday night, the boys get drunk, hoon 'round town, police give chase, boys can't make the corner, car hits tree, three dead.

We see the puer in the crocodile riders, lion tamers, snake handlers, and elephant trainers. Watching from a superior human distance, wrapped in the fantasy that they have a special relationship with a wild animal, that only they know how to whisper, how to get it under control. The more distant they are from their own human ordinariness the more inhuman the animal they are drawn to. These are the ones who bypass the warmth of bears and lions and proudly court sharks and snakes. Until, one day, the animal turns and stings, tramples, bites or savages. The right position would be to be rightly terrified, to leave it alone and not trespass on its raw Artemis-nature, to honour its mana, to give it respect, to know that it is wild and has its own kingdom.

The puer likes the virginal, the frontier, the lands undiscovered, the never-been-done-before, the unconquered, no rules, no government, no limitations. He likes life at a distance, outside, airy and pure. He hates inside, up close, sweaty, committed—there he can't breathe, needs space, feels claustrophobic, tied down. He likes to watch but not participate. The puer can't see past age 40, or even 30. He is not given to patience and working through. There is either youth or old age, with nothing in between. And he hopes he dies before he gets old.

Saturn

The archetype of the puer is not singular. It is bipolar and duplex—meaning the stick always has two ends. One end is the puer or puella, the other end is the senex or seneca (Latin for old man or woman, as in senior, senator and senile). The puer, like all of us, inevitably dies. But this death may not be a physical one, it may be a slow psychological death, where the puer turns into his opposite, the senex, the grumpy, belief-ridden old man.

The puer wants to do what's never been done before. To do this he must over-enthusiastically reject the old forms and limitations of the tried and true. All things are possible be it athletic achievement, danger, drugs or poetry. The puer flies high. His dimension is vertical and he chafes at having to adapt to the flat-earth, horizontal world. He's often creative and artistic but not always. Whenever we make order and pattern, when life is not as fresh as it used to be, when things begin to repeat themselves as they start to do in our twenties, then the senex enters. The puer rails against this, kicks and screams, and strives ever onwards and upwards. But in his desperation to escape he strengthens, in equal proportion, the downward and inward pull toward order, stasis, death and decay.

The medieval alchemists called this force Saturn and his element was lead. Slow, grinding, boring, ruminant, pedantic and ordered, he was known as the governor of the prison. He is tradition-bound, nostalgic, slow, burdened, and worldly. He is suspicious of hunches and intuitions, he like facts, solid reality, authority, knowledge, confirmation, and replicable studies. Senex pathology is excessively conservative, authoritarian, over-grounded, melancholic and lacking in imagination. But positive senex can offer mentoring, balance, humility, wisdom, life experience and far-sightedness. Art is puer, science is senex.

Friedrich Nietzsche, the German philosopher, wrote his first book, *The Birth of Tragedy from the Spirit of Music*, at age 27. In this exploration of Greek drama he wrote of the difference between the Apollonian and the Dionysian.

Apollo was the Greek god of sun and light. Dionysus was the god of wine, madness and ecstasy. Nietzsche refers to Schopenhauer's concept of the principium individuationis (principle of individuation) whereby Apollonian man separates himself from the undifferentiated substance of nature. The Dionysian impulse, in contrast, features non-rationality and immersion in the wholeness of nature. Rather than the detached, rational stance of the Apollonian, the Dionysian, which is best realised in music and dance, involves a frenzied participation in life itself. When we journey out of the Dionysian pursuits of our twenties we see, looming on the horizon, the Apollonian responsibilities of career, family, job or whatever we imagine adulthood holds in store for us. For hardcore Dionysiacs this looks like a wasteland.

In astrology, the Saturn return influences a person's life development at 28–30 year intervals. These intervals or "returns" coincide with the approximate time it takes the planet Saturn to make one orbit around the sun, that is, 29.4 years. As Saturn returns to the degree in its orbit occupied at the time of birth, a person crosses over a major threshold and enters the next stage of life. With the first Saturn return, a person leaves youth behind and enters adulthood. With the second return, maturity. And with the third and usually final return, a person enters wise old age. These returns occur roughly at the ages of 28–30, 56–60 and 84–90. The Moon Cycles sketch a similar pattern.

All things turn into their opposite over time. When senex comes to the fore, the puer finds himself sidelined, no longer able to make the team, no longer able to cut it, because he has committed the unforgivable sin of growing older. Bitterness and resentment rise when he becomes aware that the goals he had are now finally and irrevocably unattainable. Sometimes this leads to broken relationships, violence or even suicide.

On August 7, 2004 Marc Cécillon, French rugby international, shot his wife, Chantal, five times with a Magnum revolver, in front of about 60 guests at a birthday barbecue hosted by friends in a small village outside Lyons. The 47-year-old Cécillon, who earned 46 caps as a loose forward for France and was captain of the national rugby team five times during his 22-year career, had been drinking heavily and was said to be suffering from depression and an insane jealousy over his wife, who had asked for a divorce. The trial heard how Cécillon, described as "the calm man" of rugby, had been depressed after retiring from being a top sportsman and returning to "ordinary life." Psychiatric reports revealed a "fragile" personality in a depressed state.

Kokichi Tsuburaya (May 13, 1940 – January 9, 1968, 27 years 7 months 27 days) was the bronze medallist in the marathon at the 1964 Tokyo Olympics. The legendary Abebe Bikila of Ethiopa took the gold medal by several minutes. Tsubaraya was in second place coming into the stadium but was overtaken in the final 100 meters by Basil Heatley, an English runner who had held the world marathon record briefly before Bikila. Tsuburaya was honoured in Japan, which has a long history of marathon running, and he was expected to get a medal at the 1968 Mexico City Olympics.

Four years later, while training for Mexico City, Tsuburaya killed himself by slashing his wrist in his dormitory. He was found holding his bronze medal. Fellow marathoner Kenji Kimihara remembered Tsuburaya's comments before he committed suicide. He said, "I committed an inexcusable blunder [in 1964] in front of the Japanese people. I have to beg their pardon by running and hoisting the

Hinomaru [national flag] in Mexico." On January 9, 1968, Tsuburaya committed suicide. His suicide note said, "Sorry, can't run anymore."[9]

Wounds

The Big South Moon from 0–27 years of age is one of trust and innocence. The word innocence (Latin, in-nocere) means without hurt, which is the proper entitlement of childhood. But none of us had perfect parents and we all come out of childhood and adolescence wounded in some way. Puers are wounded and perhaps the members of the 27 Club are more wounded than most. The light side of the puer flies like Bellerophon on Pegasus, the winged horse, or soars like Mercury or Hermes with winged ankles. But the dark side is Achilles' heel, Philoctetes' rotting foot, Oedipus' swollen foot, Christ's feet nailed to the cross—all wounds in the places we touch the earth, the reality of our lives.

Like warriors, puers bleed and die too soon. Whether it's war and patriotism or peace and protest, it's all the same psychology. It just looks different. The warrior with blood-lust who can't stop the killing is the same as the puer who can't stop bleeding. He haemorrhages at the sight of death, even the idea of death. He is vegetarian and abstains from meat but, thinking he knows better, doesn't consult the animals on this. Rigidly hierarchical, he abhors the taking of animal life whilst murdering the carrots and the celery in their battery beds.

A puer has no internal authority and so is unable to impose his authority, in fact he makes a principle of this un-

---

[9] Tim Larimer, "The Agony of Defeat," *Time*, October 2, 2000, www.time.com/time/world/article/0,8599,2053776,00.html

der the guise of consensus, fairness, being non-judgemental, not interfering, or allowing others to have their space. He is limp and unable to defend himself, leaking tears and ideals. He gives himself to his art. He is both greedy and starving. He always wants more because he cannot hold and live what he has. He goes too far and tries to be and to have more than fate alots him. He has not built a psychic body strong enough to withstand his life, and so the body eventually gives up and gives out. Amy Winehouse's frail body could not hold her talent. Live fast and die young. Live young and die fast.

A contemporary example of the puer is Dr Gregory House of the television show, *House MD*.[10] The trailer for the show says: "He's troubled… He's wounded… He's a hero… He's medicine's most brilliant mind." House is an intuitive diagnostician who injects his mercurial energy into the seriousness of the senex hospital. He is lame in his right leg and walks with a cane. The puer in mythology is often lamed, crippled, or wounded in some way. Not only is House wounded physically but his psychological wounds show in his addiction to painkillers. The regular rules of the institution don't apply to him and his irresponsible, childlike behaviour is tolerated by the hospital because of his brilliant diagnostic skills.

The character of Dr Wilson provides House with the senex balance he needs to function. Wilson is responsible, self-disciplined and in control. He moderates the free-spirited, emotionally immature House. He's an oncologist, dedicating himself to the dying, a senex trait. Wilson uses his strong Apollonian analytical skills when diagnosing complex illnesses but after the work-up has been complet-

---

[10] http://metaheartcenter.squarespace.com/essay-the-senexed-heart/#_edn1.

ed, the final medical diagnosis results from House's intuitive insight, seemingly out of the blue, which solves the riddle. His spark of Dionysiac brilliance comes from a place beyond the rational Apollonian mind.

High flyers

In early 1918, World War I poet Wilfred Owen (March 18, 1893 – November 4, 1918, 25 years 7 months 18 days) wrote about the hard senex-reality of trench warfare and gas attacks:

> If you could hear, at every jolt, the blood
> Come gargling from the froth-corrupted lungs,
> Obscene as cancer, bitter as the cud
> Of vile, incurable sores on innocent tongues,—
> My friend, you would not tell with such high zest
> To children ardent for some desperate glory,
> The old Lie: *Dulce et decorum est*
> *Pro patria mori.*[11]

Owen's poems contrasted with the puer poems of Rupert Brooke (August 3, 1887 – April 23, 1915, 27 years 8 months 20 days), which romanticised patriotic death. Brooke was once described as "the most beautiful man in England... an embodiment of patriotic, youthful sacrifice." In 1914 he wrote "The Soldier" which begins:

> If I should die, think only this of me:
> That there's some corner of a foreign field
> That is for ever England.

---

[11] The Latin phrase is from the Roman poet Horace: "It is sweet and fitting to die for one's country."

On his way to the landing at Gallipoli, Brooke developed sepsis from an infected mosquito bite. He died in the afternoon of April 23, 1915 in a French hospital ship moored in a bay off the Greek island of Skyros in the Aegean Sea. As the expeditionary force had orders to depart immediately, Brooke was buried in a "foreign field," at 11 pm in an olive grove on Skyros. New Zealand and Australian readers will be aware of the significance of the time, date and destination as that of ANZAC day.

One of Brooke's admirers was John Gillespie Magee (9 June 1922 – 11 December 1941, 19 years 6 months 2 days). He is most famous for his poem popularly known as "High Flight." But its full title is "High Flight (An Airman's Ecstasy)."

Oh! I have slipped the surly bonds of earth,
And danced the skies on laughter-silvered wings;
Sunward I've climbed, and joined the tumbling mirth
Of sun-split clouds—and done a hundred things
You have not dreamed of—
wheeled and soared and swung
High in the sunlit silence. Hov'ring there
I've chased the shouting wind along, and flung
My eager craft through footless halls of air...
Up, up the long, delirious, burning blue
I've topped the wind-swept heights with easy grace
Where never lark or even eagle flew—
And, while with silent lifting mind I've trod
The high untrespassed sanctity of space,
Put out my hand, and touched the face of God.

Magee was born in Shanghai to an American father and British mother, both Anglican missionaries. Educated at

Rugby School from 1935 to 1939 he won the school's poetry prize in 1938. He was moved by the roll of honour of Rugby students who had fallen in the First World War. This list included Brooke who had also won the same poetry prize thirty-four years before.

Magee and his family visited the United States in 1939. However, due to the outbreak of war, he was unable to return to Britain for his final year. In October 1940 he enlisted in the Royal Canadian Air Force. He was stationed at St Catharines, Ontario, and then Ottawa. In June 1941 he was sent to Britain. While stationed at RAF Llandow, Wales, Magee wrote "High Flight."

On August 18, 1941 he had flown up to 33,000 feet in a Spitfire Mk I, his seventh flight in a Spitfire. As he climbed upward he was struck with the inspiration of a poem, "To touch the face of God." He completed it later that day after landing. Several phrases, including "touched the face of God," were likely taken from a Cuthbert Hicks poem written three years earlier.[12]

The poem has endured as a favourite among aviators and astronauts. Today it serves as the official poem of the Royal Canadian Air Force and the Royal Air Force. It must be recited from memory by fourth class cadets (freshmen) at the United States Air Force Academy (USAFA). Portions of this poem appear on many headstones in Arlington National Cemetery. Astronaut Michael Collins brought an index card with the poem typed on it on his Gemini 10 flight and included the complete poem in his autobiography *Carrying the Fire*. Ronald Reagan quoted from the poem in his speech following the Challenger disaster on January 28, 1986.

---

[12] Rupert De la Bère (1938) *Icarus: An Anthology of the Poetry of Flight*. London: Macmillan.

The hugely successful 1970 disaster movie *Airport*, based on the novel by Arthur Hailey, spawned a number of movies in that genre in the 1970s including *The Towering Inferno* which we shall come to later. The movie focuses on an airport manager trying to keep his airport open during a snow storm, while a suicidal bomber plots to blow up a Boeing 707. The epigraph used in Hailey's novel was the first two lines of Magee's poem.

Over the years the poem has struck the archetypal chord of the puer—the brave, young, beautiful and talented god who loves his country, family and flag and dies an early sacrificial death, for the good of all, selfless and patriotic. As noble and necessary as the proud tradition of the warrior might be, the archetype is not so sentimental and is not at all choosy who it kills—rock star, soldier or athlete.

The archetype wants the transformation, the death, the change, and then new life to be born. It will take any kind of death. It's not fussy if it's physical death or symbolic death. And the means don't matter either—intentional, accidental, cancer, heart attack, hanging, car accident, overdose, natural causes or suicide—all are acceptable.

Hubris

Those whom the Gods would destroy, they first call promising. —Cyril Connolly

The puer gods like Icarus, Phaeton, Prometheus and Lucifer are usually described as rebellious, prideful, full of hubris, defiant, and reckless. The Greek word hubris (Latin, superbia) means extreme haughtiness, pride or arrogance. Hubris often indicates a lack of social and emotional reality-testing and an overestimation of one's own competence or capabilities. Donald Trump is hubris on the hoof. Superbia was considered the most serious of the seven deadly sins and the source of the other sins. Lucifer's superbia and his desire to compete with Dad led to his fall from heaven. Nowadays, we think of superb as just another superlative.

Daedalus was the father of Icarus and the master craftsman who constructed the labyrinth that housed the fearsome Minotaur, and was imprisoned by King Minos in a tower to prevent him sharing the secrets of the labyrinth. He could not leave Crete by sea as the king searched all the vessels so he set about making wings for himself and his young son, Icarus. He tied feathers together with string and wax giving his wings a gentle curvature, just like the wings of a bird.

Ready to escape from Crete having equipped himself and his son, Daedalus warned Icarus not to fly too high, because the heat of the sun would melt the wax, nor too low, because the sea foam would soak the feathers. They had passed Samos and Delos by the time Icarus, forgetting his father's warning, began to soar upward toward the sun. The heat of the sun softened the wax in his wings, they fell off and he plunged into the sea and drowned.

Phaeton, the son of the nymph Clymene, boasted that his father was the sun-god Helios. Phaeton went to his father who swore to give Phaeton anything he asked for in order to prove his paternity. Phaeton wanted to drive Helios' chariot (the sun) for a day. Helios tried to dissuade Phaeton saying that not even Zeus, the king of gods, would dare drive it, as the chariot was fiery hot and the horses breathed flames. Phaeton was adamant but once in the chariot was unable to control the fierce horses when they sensed a weaker hand and the earth was in danger of burning up until Phaeton was killed by a thunderbolt from Zeus to prevent further disaster.

Nemesis was the spirit of divine retribution visited upon those who showed hubris and arrogance before the gods. She was the goddess of revenge. The word nemesis originally meant the apportionment of fortune, neither good nor bad, each according to their fate. Later, nemesis came to mean the disturbance of this right proportion and the sense of injustice which could not allow it to pass unpunished.

In WWII the Japanese coined the term for another kind of hubris, "victory disease." After the initial successes of Pearl Harbour and other victories in the Pacific in 1941, the Japanese navy suffered a catastrophic defeat at the Battle of Midway in 1942. Victory disease refers to the complacency or arrogance brought on by a victory which results in disastrous defeat.

But victory disease was around well before WWII. In 1314, the overconfidence and lack of preparation by Edward II (The Hammer of the Scots) led to his disastrous defeat by the Scots led by Robert the Bruce at the Battle of Bannockburn. In 1415, at the Battle of Agincourt, the English were grossly outnumbered by five to one, but the arrogance of the French knights, and accuracy of the English longbows, led to the rout of the French. Disastrously, Napoleon invaded Russia in 1812 with a force of about 600,000 French soldiers, of which about 40,000 returned. In 1879, at the Battle of Isandlwana, Zulu warriors equipped mainly with spears and shields defeated British forces armed with modern firearms and artillery. In 1941 Hitler invaded the Soviet Union in Operation Barbarossa. He underestimated Soviet military resilience, counted on the success of old tactics, was confident of quick victory, and did not count on getting caught in the Russian winter or rasputitsa (mud season). Millions died on both sides.

Grief

One of the tasks in the west of all the Little Moons and for the whole Big West Moon (39–42) is to become acquainted with grief. We grow through loss. But we resist both. Beginning in our late twenties and through our thirties we are caught between the escape velocity of adolescent enthusiasm and the increasing gravitational pull of our forties. We need to be disappointed as much as we need to be inspired and it's between the hammer and the anvil of these experiences that we are forged.

Creative people who are pueri or puellae must be strong enough to accept both their greatness and their weakness, otherwise they get torn apart. They have experiences that are so deep and broad and full of life that it is hard let go of them when their time has passed. The essence of an experience that is alive, orgastic and numinous is that it never comes again in the same way. The pattern is unique and although archetypal experience repeats itself, its form changes. If one does not sacrifice the experience after it occurs then it remains as a pull toward death. The more one waits for, or grabs for a repeat of the same experience the more it recedes and one is left with a sense of the water of life ebbing away.

Like Icarus we must fall back to earth and into what this particular life is about. Not someone else's life, someone else's dreams, but my life, my successes and my failures. We must let go of the dreams, the aspirations, and the heroics. But this natural movement goes against the grain—we get lots of encouragement going up but are usually abandoned coming down. "Higher, faster! Live your dreams! You can become anything you want! All things are possible! Gimme another rocket! Waddya mean, we've run out! Oh, you're depressed are you? Wassa matter? You've got lots to be grateful for."

I dramatise, but not nearly enough. We get time to adjust and a decade is a long time for the letting go. For billions of us this all happens under the skin of life and we don't see it except when it breaks out in the rashes and sores of relationships, bankruptcy, illness, violence or suicide. All these deaths are a pale substitute, a measly sacrifice, paltry alms in place of the real burnt offering that is the death of the dreams, hopes, wishes, and the longings of our twenties.

If we do not bring about death and change consciously (and who does, easily?) then it will happen in a concrete, literal way—there will be a death through an overdose for the rock star, paralysis for the athlete, head injury for the academic, blindness for the painter, throat surgery gone wrong for the singer. What is denied in the invisible world perforce must happen in the visible world. If the wound of loss is not allowed then it will slit us open.

Tony Kushner wrote in *Angels in America*: "How do people change?… God splits the skin with a jagged thumbnail from throat to belly and then plunges a huge filthy hand in, he grabs hold of your bloody tubes… And then he stuffs them back, dirty, tangled and torn. It's up to you to do the stitching." If you are unable tolerate anything less, you die. And the anything less may be too much. Death may be the easier course.

I sketch this rather starkly because the collective turns away from such notions. Yes, sometimes shit just happens and we are in the wrong place at the wrong time. But there are other factors at work besides the old favourites—coincidence, accident, and pure chance.

Suicide

> Then I overdosed at 28, at which point I began to accept the bipolar diagnosis. —Carrie Fisher

> Suicide is what the death certificate says when one dies of depression. —Peter D. Kramer

There are four types of suicide and each has a different relationship to life and death. The first type is afraid of both life and death. They are always playing on the edge and taking extreme risks at sports, sex, drugs or relationships, as a way of denying, conquering or "managing" their fear. In equal measure they are also turned on by life and death, and often death comes by "accident." Death can snuff out a life that strays too close to the edge or falls asleep at the wheel. Most of the 27 Club belong to this type.

The second is afraid of death. This person often leave notes or clues, has had frequent incomplete para-suicidal attempts or a history of attempts before completion. Some of the 27 Club belong to this type.

The third is afraid of neither life nor death. During the samurai era in Japan, seppuku was respected as a means of atonement for failure; in the Hindu funeral practice of sati, now outlawed, a widow was expected to immolate herself on her husband's funeral pyre; self-immolation has also been practised by Tibetan monks; Japanese kamikaze flyers deliberately crashed their planes into enemy targets; and terrorist suicide bombers blow themselves up. None of the 27 Club belong to this type.

The fourth is afraid of life. Life has become too painful as in the case of those with a history of trauma, or end-of-life assisted suicides, or terminal illness euthanasia. Some of the 27 Club belong to this type.

I include the following quote, with respect, as a profoundly raw statement from a suicide forum. I do not know what happened to the young man speaking here.

I had a good childhood. Even though my parents beat me and psychologically tormented me, I was strong enough as a kid to preserve my own sanity in the midst of insane surroundings. But now, at 25, the manifestations of my parent's style of upbringing are undeniable. I crave close relationships with people around me but because of the pain associated with close relationships.... I have no real friends I can have a deep conversation with. Receiving beating after beating at the hand of my dad, only to be told afterward that it was because he loved me has scarred me so deeply that any talk of love brings up feelings of disgust and revenge, and has prevented me from doing things which could be called "nice" for other people.

I have become the most despicable person I know, and rather than look out for the interests of others, I can only cheat or steal from others to get what I want. I don't even know what I want out of life any more. It used to be a good job, then it was a girlfriend, then peace of mind, but I can't even see the point in any of these any more.... So, I give myself just under 2 years to live. If I have been able to make some radical change to my life by the time I'm 27 then so be it, I'll live another few years, but if not—I'm going out.

Hopefully by then they'll have developed a better way of making a peaceful pill which doesn't require owning a fucking science laboratory.[13]

Questions

The puer is a problem for all of us and the question is this: *How can I grow up while retaining the feeling of wholeness, creativity, excitement, and aliveness I had in my youth?* But this statement has something of the puer about it. So the question may be: *Can I relinquish the things of my youth in exhange for the gifts of middle age?* If not, excitement becomes depression. These questions become more urgent toward the end of our twenties—the Moon Cycles say around 27—then we spend the next 27 years answering them.

Life is kind—it gives us lots of time to adjust and mostly we don't notice either the question or the answer, as they happen inch by inch, day by day. But the puer who hangs onto the past and resists the future may be unable to undergo the necessary death and change of the Big West Moon between 27 and 54. He may hang on to material symbols of youth (physical accomplishments, possessions, sport, women, and money).

The inexorable shift as we grow older is from matter to spirit, from material gain to spiritual gain. The tide comes in for the first half of life and goes out in the second half. In his attempt to swim against the outgoing tide of life the puer is unable to exchange one satisfaction for the other. The tide turns between ages 39–42 (the Little West Moon of the Big West Moon, the time of double death and change) and particularly at age 40.6 (the west of the Little West Moon of the Big West Moon, the place of triple death and change).

---

[13] suicideproject.org/2011/08/joinng-the-27-club/

So it is around age 27 that the puer sets his course for the next 27 years of the Big West Moon, the moon of death and change. Three ways to go here. First, physical death. The 27 Club members die then and there. Second, others die psychologically, with physical death coming later. Third, others make the necessary deaths and sacrifices along the way—of youth, of dreams, of loves. Those whose fate it is to stay the course until age 54 find that, though the fifties are the old age of youth, they are also the youth of old age and bring great reward.

The recipe for admission to the 27 Club is part historical circumstance (the sixties were a prime time for young death), part occupation (rock 'n' roll is a high risk profession), part the burden of genius (the personality and the body must be strong to carry the voltage), and part personal history (if Jim Morrison's father had not been who he was; if Jimi Hendrix's mother had not been alcoholic; if Kurt Cobain's family had not split up when he was young).

The outer facts of their lives apparently tell us a lot but really offer very little. They do not tell us what happened in the psyche of these people which may have led to their death. Many millions of others have similar histories, and much worse, but have not died and indeed may have thrived. Rarely do we know anything of the ones who did not die physically at age 27 but died spiritually or emotionally around that age. One biographer described the tragic life of Skip Spence, the Canadian-born guitarist for Moby Grape, who died homeless after many years of mental illness and drug addiction, as one who "neither died young nor had a chance to find his way out."[14]

Then there are those from the sixties who continued on to live full and productive lives. Amazingly, Keith Richards

---

[14] en.wikipedia.org/wiki/Skip_Spence.

is still alive. Mick Jagger is still as full of life as he was at 27 and, while Jim Morrison was dying in Paris, Paul McCartney was rejuvenating on the Mull of Kintyre.

Drew Grant said, "If you want to come out of this [the 27 Club] with one theory, it's that when the expectations reach a fever pitch, it becomes its own disease. Not to get all smoke monster on it, but I'm only half-bullshitting when I say I think it's going to take the weak ones first."[15]

---

[15] www.salon.com/entertainment/tv/
feature/2011/07/26/27_club_curse_or_myth.

2

Rhythm and Pattern

Life must be lived forwards but can only be understood backwards. —Soren Kierkegaard

The first half of life consists of the capacity to enjoy without the chance; the last half consists of the chance without the capacity. —Mark Twain

The first half of life is spent in longing for the second, the second half in regretting the first.

—French Proverb

The first half of life is devoted to forming a healthy ego, the second half is going inward and letting go of it. —C. G. Jung

One happens. Two is coincidence. Three is pattern.

—Anon.

All things have rhythm and pattern. Everything has a heartbeat, a voice, a song and a dance. The physical body has its rhythms and patterns. Our heart beats, we sleep 8 hours out of 24, cells grow and replace themselves in rhythm, pregnancy is 9 months long. We would notice if we slept two hours a night one week and ten hours a night the next week. Or if pregnancy was ten months long for some women and six months for other women. But we take our obvious biological rhythms for granted and have become insulated from the more subtle rhythms of the seasons, the psyche, and the stars. The human psyche has rhythms like the body. It's just that we have forgotten, to our peril. Like the body, the psyche has its own inbuilt sense of balance and when we get too one-sided or seriously out of step with its natural rhythms we invite correction and compensation. Goethe said, "We must always change, renew, rejuvenate ourselves, otherwise, we harden." And when things harden they get brittle and crack.

This book is about an archetypal rhythm of the psyche that can be understood through the Moon Cycles. It teaches us about the inevitable rhythms of our lives and the importance of the 9 month, 3 year, and 27 year cycles.

Archetypes

The hero-warrior, die-with-your-boots-on, freedom-bent young man of either gender who rushes romantically, sentimentally or angrily into the arms of death for the sake of his music-art-freedom-country is a familiar pattern. But when our lives follow a pattern overly much we lose our freedom even though we may think that's the very thing we are fighting for. Jung called these patterns archetypes. Myths and fairy tales are the great stories that archetypes give rise to. Myth, Jung said, is not fiction. It consists of facts that are continually repeated and can be observed over and over again.

Some examples? The tyrannical ruler, the tortured genius, the mad scientist, the doomed romantic, the geeky teenager, the jealous lover, the brave soldier, the funny clown, or the wise man. They are the stuff of front-page news, sentimental admiration, stand-up comedy and cartoon stereotypes. They are millennia-old patterns of human behaviour that have sedimented into recognisable forms of human conduct. They are the channel dug, for example, by the age-old river of falling in love. Over tens, even hundreds of thousands of years it has carved a waterway that we willingly fall headlong into and are swept down to the sea. Some learn to swim, others drown.

Jung said that to find the treasure, the diamond of oneself, one must free oneself from the demands of the instincts on the one hand and the tyranny of the archetypes on the other. Both rob us of our inner gold. The psyche wants us to become ourselves.

Humans are hard-wired to notice patterns. There are millions of patterns but they are so everyday that they become invisible to us—we take them for granted. Or they only appear if we look for them. Some patterns occur in the visible world of matter (and attract the interest of science) some in the world of spirit, invisible to the senses.

After something happens to us for "the first time" we have to have noticed it, it must have registered in some way in our consciousness for it to be recognisable when it occurs a second time. Someone must have noticed that more than one rock star has died at age 27. So we begin to count: first, second. This is the beginning of human consciousness. Now things are split into first and second. This is the simplest pattern and it is created by division. One splits into two—before and after, this and that, back and front, then and now.

So it is with life. And here's our first pattern. First half. Second half. In the first half of life we add, grow, multiply, increase, learn and develop. Death is not on the horizon. We are innocent, naive, unaware, bullet-proof and gung-ho. But in the second half of life less is more. We grow through loss—shedding and stripping away what is superfluous so that what is at the centre can be more clearly seen. If we have lost our inner compass, if we are more than four steps away from our inner community, then the Self will nudge us, cajole, us, warn us, or startle us either in our waking life or in our dream life. In the courts of law, ignorance is no defence. So it is with nature; sooner or later we pay for the offense of not being known to ourselves. The 27 Club got the ultimate wake-up call.

But first and second are static, there is no movement, no children, no multiplication. The pattern that moves and grows is the number 3. The first 1 and the second 1 come together to create a third 1. Mother-father-child. The punch line of a joke is often about the third recurrence of a situation. Events in fairy tales happen in threes. The third time is lucky. If something happens once it is a unique event. When a second event happens, it's noticed if it is similar to the first time, but it could also be "coincidence." But when it happens a third time and it is similar to the previous two times then three events are often beyond coincidence and are confirmation that there is a pattern at work here, something is moving. The event has come into space in the first instance, the second instance gives it duration in time, and in the third instance it has three dimensions—time, space and form.

The Moon Cycles are a pattern—a regularly recurring cycle of events that occur over the course of our lives. It is not a humanly constructed rhythm but a rhythm of life that is noticeable if we just look. They have a rhythm in threes that goes:

First, 9 months, a pregnancy, the time it takes for something to grow.

Second, 3 years, which is four pregnancies, the time it takes for something to grow to completion.

Third, 27 years, which is 9 cycles of 3 years, the time it takes something to come back to the place where it started and to begin a new spiral.

Then the same rhythm of 3 repeats itself with the Big Moons. The first 27 years (0–27) is life experience, the first time around. The second 27 years (27–54) is the repetition of that experience so we can learn and understand our life pattern. The third 27 years (54–81) is the distillation and extraction of wisdom from our learning in the first 54 years.

We see a similar rhythm in psychotherapy where clients will begin to make deeper changes after 9 months in therapy. Also any major life change (death, retirement, immigration, for example) takes 3 years to work through. The first year is mourning, the second year is thinking that we are over the loss, the third year is realising we aren't and coming to terms with the changes and consolidating a new identity. In couples therapy we notice that new relationships often run into trouble after about 18 months (two pregnancies) which is half-way (the place of death and change in the west) around the first Little Moon of the relationship.

The purpose of life is to become who we are. To become our own person. Not the family's person, the culture's person or the archetype's person (as important as these are along the way) but our own person. Then we have a personality, we become an original, a one-off. This is our gift, our medicine, our give-away to the collective. This individuality is what heals and corrects the social norm when it needs a shake-up. But up until age 27 the situation is reversed. We are still an apprentice to life, we have to adapt to the culture we live in, and find a place in society. If we have too much individuality too soon, the collective norm corrects those who exceed themselves—or it kills them.

The pattern of who we are is unique. Never before has the one-off combination of atoms, molecules, DNA, hair, fingerprints, voice, face, feelings, tastes, attitudes, and personality ever existed, and it will never exist again. So our life-path is made up of a triangle: One, what we are given from the start. Two, what we get as we go along. Three, what we make of those two. Although our uniqueness is, er, unique, it's also common. Everyone has it, potentially anyway. Why is uniqueness so important? Because it too is a pattern, but it's a pattern that will never be repeated.

So how do we know what is most truly ourselves? How do we answer the question, "Who am I?" Well, the answer is never what you think. Jung had some thoughts about this. He said that the human psyche has an organising centre which he called the Self or the God-image within. Shortly before his death, he said to the soldier and writer Sir Laurens van der Post, "I cannot define for human beings what God is, but what I can say is that my scientific work has proved the pattern of God exists in every human being. And that this pattern has at its disposal the greatest transforming energies of which life is capable."[16]

---

[16] Quoted in a book review by Valerie Harms of Nancy Ryley, *The Forsaken Garden: Four Conversations on the Deep Meaning*

The Self reveals itself through dreams on the inside and through synchronicity on the outside. But we have to pay attention or else we miss the signs. Dreams are our inner compass that guides us through the maze and wrong turns of our beliefs, our upbringing, our education, and our relationships, to the ever-changing but solid ground of our own nature. Yes, bad things do happen to good people but catastrophic life events are more likely to occur when we have lost our compass.

In the first half of life we look to the collective norms of the group we live in. "Am I normal?" "Do I belong?" "Am I meeting the expectations (of compliance, of rebellion), doing my job, doing the right thing?" This is as it should be for the first 27 years of life. We must fit in, belong, conform, get a job, get an education, abide by the rules (even if it is the rules of a counter-culture). We must find a place in society and contribute to the common wealth. In other words, our job is to become a useful human being.

For most people, life stops there or thereabouts. Married, 2.2 children, and a steady job (replace with your gender-cultural-religious preference). Although we can't go there in this book, the so-called mid-life crisis around age forty is meant to shake this up.

Those rock stars who died in their late twenties are the poster children, a tragically visible markers, for the end of the first Big Moon of the Moon Cycles. At age 27 we move from the Big South Moon of childhood into the Big West Moon of adolescence. Then at age 54 we go into the Big North Moon of adulthood. (Yes, that's right, we only become an adult in our mid-fifties.) And then into the Big East Moon of elderhood at 81.

of *Environmental Illness*, Wheaton: IL, Quest, 1998, cgjungpage. org/articles/harmseview.html.

But remember that 27 is a stage not an age. Physical death is not inevitable at 27. It is not a "curse" any more than a heart attack is inevitable at 54. It's just a rhythm, strong for some, weak for others. And, if we listen to the feedback from what happens to us, life usually goes better.

For example, Jack White (born July 9, 1975) of the White Stripes was in a car accident on July 11, 2003 with his erstwhile girlfriend Renee Zellweger. He suffered a compound fracture of his index finger which prevented him from playing guitar and he had to cancel his European tour. He was two days past his 28th birthday. After surgery White wrote, "lots of pain, typing with one finger, made it through a year of rock n' roll death, got off with just a warning."[17]

The "death" at 27 may be a symbolic death—of an idea, a relationship, a movement, a job, or even a band. Paul McCartney was born on June 18, 1942. The last time all four Beatles were in a recording studio together, to record the last of the Beatles albums, Abbey Road, was on August 20, 1969. McCartney was aged 27 years, 2 months and 2 days.

On November 27, 1970 George Harrison released a solo album *All Things Must Pass*, a collection of songs, including "The Art of Dying," which he had written over his years with the Beatles. He was 27 years, 9 months and 2 days

Cat Stevens was born Steven Georgiou on July 21, 1948 to a Greek-Cypriot father and a Swedish mother. In 1976 (he was likely aged late-27 but some reports date the event as 1975) Stevens was staying at the house of Jerry Moss, his American record boss, at Malibu Beach:

> I decided to go for a swim. Of course, nobody told me that it wasn't a good time to go swimming.... And then I tried to swim back to shore. And suddenly I

---

[17] http://www.whitestripes.net/faq.php

felt 'I can't do this'—the tide was going the other way. I wasn't getting any closer. Suddenly I was petrified. I thought: 'This might be it.' I said: 'God, if you save me, I'll work for you.' It was without hesitation that I knew that, instinctively, there was a power that could help me. And then a little wave, you know, came behind me—a little wave, it wasn't very big. But it was that miraculous moment when suddenly the tide was going in my favour. I had my energy, I could swim back. I was on land. I was alive.[18]

He later said, "I had to deflate myself. I had to come back to life."[19] His brush with death intensified his long-held quest for spiritual truth and he later converted to Islam.

Echoes and ripples

All events that occur now have happened before and each occurrence, individual or collective, impresses its energetic form and weight on the other world to reinforce the pattern. The form of the pattern is recognisable although the details are different each time.

Time is not a line, it is a sphere and the ripples set off by decisions and events in our lives radiate out in all eight directions, "forwards" into the future, and "backwards" into the past. These waves in turn combine with other waves to create new archetypal patterns and modify existing ones. So I invite the reader to play with time, and not be overly burdened by linearity and precision. Allowing a generous distance from the details enables us to see the rhythms and patterns of which the 27 Club is a part.

[18] Yusuf Islam Reflects On His Return. CBS News. www.cbsnews.com/2100-3445_162-2221286.html

[19] www.foxnews.com/story/0,2933,237698,00.html

The Moon Cycles can be applied to any important event, not just the human lifespan, and we can follow the tracks of an event forwards or backwards in time. The birth and death of anything follows the Moon Cycles, particularly in 27- or 54-year rhythms.

For example: Hollywood dreams for Western culture. Just like our own dreams at night, Hollywood shows us images of what's happening in the collective psyche. These rarely "come true" in the literal sense but they point to an archetypal current moving underneath the surface. The more we ignore our dreams and the feedback they provide to our waking consciousness, the more likely their emotional themes will actualise on our waking lives.

The tragedy of 9/11 and the destruction of the two towers of the World Trade (sic) Centre was, amongst many other things, an obvious sign that the global economic house of cards would collapse, twice. And would probably collapse twice a number of times. What was born on September 11, 2001 will begin its Big Chaotic Journey in 2028.

If we look 27 years backwards from 9/11 we find something interesting. *The Towering Inferno*, starring Steve McQueen and Paul Newman, was the biggest motion picture of the 1974-75 season. The film was based on *The Tower*, a 1973 novel by Richard Martin Stern. He was inspired to write the novel by the construction of the World Trade Centre! It opened on April 4, 1973. In the novel, a bomb in the utility room of a 138-floor tower (the world's tallest) causes a power surge which sets a janitor's closet on fire. On 9/11 the first plane hit the North Tower between the 92nd and 98th floors. The second plane hit the South Tower between the 78th and 94th floors. In the movie, people escape from the top floor by breeches buoy to the adjacent 110-story North Tower of the World Trade Centre, but it is only partially successful. More than a hundred partygoers die in the restaurant on the top floor.

The movie started filming on May 8, 1974 and, wait for it, finished filming on September 11, 1974, exactly 27 years before 9/11.[20] The film's opening credits included a dedication which read: "To those who give their lives so that others might live, to the firefighters of the world, this picture is gratefully dedicated." All pure coincidence, I'm sure.

The Sixties

> We live in a terrible split… The danger lies in splitting the duplex into only senex or puer. We had one-sided puer in the sixties, and now that chaotic style of destruction is giving way to a programmed style of senex destruction. —James Hillman, *Inter Views*

As brilliant as Jim Morrison, Jimi Hendrix and Janis Joplin were (have we heard the likes of "The End" or "All Along the Watchtower" or "Little Piece of My Heart" since then?) they also carried the archetypal burden of the forces emerging in the sixties. The senex/puer polarisation came violently to the fore in the sixties in rock 'n' roll and the Vietnam War protests. The USA was born as a senex/puer culture. It fled the old European senex culture by a puer flight to the New World. But it brought with it the most senex of seeds in the form of its founding Puritanism. The sixties were the first time that the split was visible on such a massive social scale. ROTC vs. draft dodgers, dope vs. Vietnam.

The horrors of the 1940s had been desperately repressed, the hyper-normality of the 1950s was still smarmy and righteous, but the 1960s were an outbreak, a break

---

[20] www.imdb.com/title/tt0072308/trivia

out. "Don't trust anyone over 30" was the prescient phrase. Seeing as we all grow older, it was a self-annihilating, even suicidal, affirmation. The urge for individuation, released from the shackles of war, and its co-dependent, narcotising partner, peace, was projected onto the counter-culture. "Tune in, turn on, drop out," said Timothy Leary. Communes, dope, acid and Woodstock.

As with any archetypal possession, everything got too high or too low, and something had to give. Whenever a form splits, be it a cultural form, a political movement, an historical era, or a scientific theory, it splits violently otherwise it is just a rearrangement of the old form and nothing new will be born. When it does split the imagination explodes, possibilities abound and the puer soars high.

The beatnik, coffee-house, folk music culture of the 1950s segued into the hippie era which began in the early sixties with, for example, Ken Kesey and his Merry Pranksters. The brief "Summer of Love" in Haight-Ashbury, San Francisco in 1967 lasted for about 3 years. The high point was Woodstock in late August 1969 which was hard on the heels of the Tate-LaBianca murders by Charles Manson in early August.

Then came the shootings at Kent State in May 1970, the killing at the Stones' Altamont concert in December 1970, the bombing of Cambodia, and things began to crumble. Jimi Hendrix's last UK concert was at the Isle of Wight Festival in late August 1970 and he was dead a few weeks later. Janis Joplin died in her hotel room in October 1970. Jim Morrison moved to Paris in March 1971.

So what happened 27 or 54 years before this period? We find that the turmoil that was the late 60s and early 70s was the first Big Chaotic Journey of World War II (1939–1945) which passed through between 1966–1972. Going further back we find that WWII itself was the first Big Chaotic Journey of World War I (1914–1918) which ran from 1941–1945 and its second Big Chaotic Journey ran from 1968–1972!

We hear the same rhythm in the history of rock. The hippie hair had become too long, the jeans too unwashed, then glam rock, in turn, became just too much, so punk was born in the mid-1970s—about 27 years after the birth of rock 'n' roll itself in the late 1940s. After that, grunge was born in the late 1980s–early 1990s, 27 years after the second wave of rock began in the late 1960s.

Nine

Now, if 6 turned up to be 9,
I don't mind, I don't mind....
I've got my own life to live
I'm the one that's gonna have to die
When it's time for me to die
So let me live my life the way I want to.
— Jimi Hendrix, "If 6 was 9," *Axis: Bold as Love*

Each Big Moon of 27 years is made up of 9 Little Moons of 3 years each. Nine is important in understanding the Moon Cycles so let's look at its meaning and symbolism of the number 9.

Energy moves in ten movements or transformations beginning at 0 and moving outward 9 times before returning to the source (10) to begin a new cycle. Note that 0 to 9 is a ten-step movement (0–1–2–3–4–5–6–7–8–9) just as, more conventionally, we might count from 1 to 10. Each form is born at 0, transforms itself 9 times, and at 10 becomes the zero of the next cycle.

The first seven steps are the development of pattern; at the eighth step the pattern is completed and at the ninth step the pattern breaks apart, creating chaos so that it can return to the source and re-create itself anew. At this 9th movement energy turns around, creates a chaotic pattern and returns to the completion of 10.

The number 9 is about timing, knowing when to stop, when to start, when to watch and when to act. It is the ability to use our energy most efficiently ("a stitch in time saves nine") to catch the opportunities and lucky breaks offered by the chaos of life.

Nine is the highest point attainable by a single number and is the last number before the return to the unity of the 10. It associates to timing and the maximum imaginable as in, "dressed to the nines," "on cloud nine," "the whole nine yards," "nine times out of ten," "a nine-day wonder," or "possession is nine-tenths of the law." Tiresias the seer told Zeus that a woman had nine times as much sexual pleasure as a man. In medieval Wales a dog that had bitten someone could be killed if it was nine steps away from its owner's house, and nine people assaulting one constituted a genuine attack. In German law the ownership of land terminated after the ninth generation. In Mayan the number nine means "to stop, to detain, to limit."

We see the number nine in pregnancy. The mother has the potential to become pregnant (0), she then receives the seed (1), becomes pregnant (2), gives birth after nine months (9), and then returns to 0 again but with a separate other, the baby (1+0). After nine months in the womb, we start at the 0 of 10 again.

Nine is a recursive number—in other words it always returns to itself. All nine digits add up to nine (1 + 2 + 3 + 4 + 5 + 6 + 7 + 8 + 9 = 45 = 9). Nine added to itself is nine (9

+ 9 = 18 = 9). Nine multiplied by itself is nine (9 x 9 = 81 = 9). Nine multiplied by any number always equals nine (9 x 7 = 63 = 6 + 3 = 9; 9 x 22 = 198 = 1 + 9 + 8 = 9).

In a circle there are four cardinal and four non-cardinal directions plus the centre which equals nine. In the Hindu tradition the number 9 is considered a complete, perfected and divine number. Nine symbolises completeness in the Bahai faith. In the Christian angelic hierarchy there are nine choirs of angels. At the ninth hour of the crucifixion Christ asked God why he had forsaken him. Ramadan, the month of fasting and prayer, is the ninth month of the Islamic calendar. The initiatory Eleusinian Mysteries took nine days. The Romans buried their dead on the ninth day and held a feast, the Novennalia, every ninth year in memory of the dead. Yggdrasil, the World Tree, had nine roots plunging into nine springs, and the nine branches reached toward the nine heavens. Odin hung from the World Tree for nine days and nine nights before he received the wisdom of the Runes. There were Nine Circles of Hell in Dante's Divine Comedy. The River Styx encircled Hades nine times. There are nine planets. A cat is pregnant for nine weeks and has nine lives. There are nine months of pregnancy. Each of the Big Moon Cycles reduces to a 9 (27, 54, 81 and 135).

Jung described nine this way: "Unless the conscious mind intervened, the unconscious would go on sending out wave after wave without result, like the treasure that is said to take nine years, nine months, and nine nights [equals 27] to come to the surface and, if not found on the last night, sinks back to start all over again from the beginning."

The debate around the 27 Club in rock music has its twin in classical music. Wikipedia opines that it is a superstitious belief that a ninth symphony is destined to be a composer's last and he or she will be fated to die after writing it, or before completing a tenth. A composer who produces a ninth symphony has reached a decisive landmark; to embark on a tenth is to challenge fate. The entry continues, sniffily, that it is a "folk-notion" found in popular journalism, and is "not supported in musicology or serious music criticism."

But, just for fun, let's look at some of the patterns. Mozart wrote 27 piano concertos. The premiere of No. 27 was Mozart's last public appearance as a performer and he died nine months later. Franz Schubert completed his Ninth Symphony and started work on his Tenth shortly before he died. Anton Bruckner died in the midst of writing his Symphony No. 9 in D minor. Antonin Dvorak's last symphony was his Symphony No. 9, likewise Ralph Vaughan Williams. Gustav Mahler completed his Ninth Symphony but died two years later with his Tenth unfinished.

In an essay on Mahler, the composer Arnold Schoenberg wrote: "It seems that the Ninth is a limit. He who wants to go beyond it must pass away. It seems as if something might be imparted to us in the Tenth which we ought not yet to know, for which we are not ready. Those who have written a Ninth stood too close to the hereafter."

Pregnancy

The Moon Cycles are based on a lunar measurement of time over the individual life span. The lunar cycle, the time between full moons, is 29.5 days. The length of pregnancy is about 39 weeks or 280 days from the beginning of the last menstrual period. However, ovulation, and usually conception, occurs 14 or 15 days into the menstrual cycle. Thus the time from conception to birth is about 266 days, which is also the number of days in 9 lunar months (9 x 29.5 = 265.5). Part of the highly sophisticated secular and spiritual Mayan calendar system is the tzolkin, which is 260 days long. Maya daykeepers say this is based on the length of human pregnancy.

The first calendars were lunar calendars of twelve months of thirty days each, but over time the lunar calendar became out-of-step with the solar year of 365¼ days. The Roman, Jewish, and Mayan calendars are lunisolar calendars, and solved the problem with intercalary days or months, added or inserted, to keep the shorter moon calendar in step with the solar year. Our modern Gregorian calendar is a solar calendar.

The Moon Cycles are expressed in the months and years of our modern Gregorian calendar and are made up of 3-year cycles; each one is a Circle of Life Experience or Little Moon. Each Little Moon is 1096 days long (3 x 365¼) which, divided up into four quadrants, makes a quarter round of 274 days. Similarly, if we divide 3 years into quarters, each quarter is three-quarters of a year. The solar year is divided into quarters by the solstices and equinoxes and the length of 3 of these quarters (for example, from December 22 to September 22) is 274 days. So the 9 months it takes to move from one cardinal direction to the next, on a Little Moon, is half-way between the length of pregnancy, as it is usually calculated (280 days), and the time from conception to birth (266 days).

Moon

The moon governs all hidden rhythms and influences: the tides, the stages of pregnancy, the menstrual cycle, the plants, the blood. It is related to the growth of plants: the full moon for leaf crops, the new moon for root crops. The moon symbolises the semi-darkness, the half-light of the unconscious, secrecy, hiddenness; it does not generate its own light but receives it from the sun, and then vanishes for 3 nights each month. From the sunny-side, lop-side of Western consciousness the moon looks dark, mad and crazy. It's all cold nights, bat-wings, howling, witches, cauldrons, spells, sleep, chaos, regression, murder, madness, secrecy, silence, and lunacy. The moon stands on the border between the light of the sun and the darkness of night and is associated with those things that live between the worlds—magic, vampires, ghosts and werewolves.

The moon is also associated with water: sap, dew, tides, the emotions. On moonlit nights dew is supposed to drip from the moon. When something is too hard, the moon brings softness, but it also brings about dissolution into madness and dismemberment when the ego is not ready for the intensity of the archetype. We can see this in the myth of Actaeon who was torn apart by his own dogs.

The moon, as the closest body to Earth, is the intermediary between Earth and other heavenly influences, and all descending influences that take on material form have to pass through the moon, thus the Virgin Mary is associated with the moon. This recognises the psychic reality that any concrete expression of our life energies belongs to the feminine principle. In other words, the feminine incarnates and gives birth.

Mythologically, the moon was said to come to earth and transform itself into a snake and have intercourse with women, or if an unmarried woman looked at the moon, she would become pregnant. Stone snakes were made to bring about women's fertility. The moon is also associated with death because it disappears every month for 3 days, and the four days of a woman's menstrual period is the hidden death cycle when the old makes way for the new. So the fertilising power of snakes, the moon's changeability, its reptilian coldness, the death and rebirth of the snake when it sheds its skin, the appearance and disappearance of snakes and the moon—all are closely associated within the moon-snake-water-death-rebirth-woman images.

Time

The moon also has a mental aspect to it. The Sanskrit root me- gave rise to such English words as moon, month, menstrual, mind, mental, measure. The Indo-European root of the word "time" is di-, meaning to cut up or divide, and is cognate with the Latin caedere, to cut through or cut off, which gives the English words decide, homicide, suicide. Thus the moon is related to the mental aspect of time as discriminated into observable units, subject to measurement, but still retaining some of its mystery.

Sun-time measures outward events that are observable in the world, while moon-time measures the timing of less visible or inner events. The first calendars were lunar calendars which measured a different kind of phenomena than the later solar calendars that supplanted them as human cultures became pastoralised. Solar calendars measure secular time and moon calendars measure sacred time. Most ecclesiastical calendars are lunar.

The moon is also closely associated with the cycles of reincarnation. For the ancient Greeks the Elysian fields, where heroes went after death, were on the moon. Plutarch wrote that after death the body (soma) was given back to the earth, the mind (nous) was given back to the sun, and the soul (psyche) was purified in the moon. Likewise, the moon is associated with spinning and weaving which in turn are associated with time; the Egyptian lunar goddess Neith invented weaving; the Moirae or the Fates were lunar goddesses who spun the fate of the individual.

When a woman is on her moon (her menstrual period) she sits directly in front of Crack-between-the-Worlds of spirit and substance. Moonlight and twilight are the times when there is a movement from spirit to substance and substance to spirit, and magic happens. This feminine, moon wisdom has respect for cosmic laws and natural cycles. The moon is about time as it is experienced in a physical, lived life. Ideals, beliefs, philosophies, intuitions, dreams and goals only become real when they enter our lives and our actions in space and time.

So the moon is about time-ing—not the hurry-up day-time of the sun but the slower twilight-time of the moon. The moon is about the capacity to look beyond linear time and wait for cyclical time, to know and live the reality that to everything there is a season, as with the Moon Cycles. It is the waiting over many years between the first insight into how life might be, or who one is, and the actual living of that reality. It is the mood of patience, waiting for things come down from the dream and manifest in the physical world.

In Western culture, time has lost its numinosity and become a secular commodity. Time is saved or spent, wasted or bought. Those who are closer to the tempo of the Self, as expressed in the natural world or in the inner world, are more aligned with Moon Cycles. The archetype of time is closely related to the rhythm of the Self, so every neurotic deviation from the Self is reflected in a disturbed relationship with time. Our culture has lost its connection with time as a link to what feeds the soul. So we have disorders of time, where time is lost, dismembered, or worshipped: dissociative disorder, attention deficit disorder, obsessive-compulsive disorder.

Those who are cut off from the natural rhythm of the human life cycle, their own body rhythms and the rhythms of the seasons and the stars, feel they are beyond time and are immortal. Or they feel that everything must be done now and they have no time at all.

Kairos and Kronos

Time reflects the doings of the Creator as seen in the rhythmic changes of the seasons and the years, the planets and stars. It is often represented by several gods or goddesses, each representing a different aspect of time. In Greek mythology there is Oceanos or Cronos, the god of time as the river or ocean; Nike, the goddess of the moment of balance between victory and defeat; Kairos, the god of the opportune moment; and the Moirae, the goddesses of fate. The Maya have the year-lords and the day-gods. Buddha meditated under the banyan tree for one lunar cycle before he attained enlightenment. For indigenous cultures, time is numinous; it is a way of staying aligned with the rhythms of the Creator. Time's orderedness, observed over centuries, gives an understanding as to how the movement between substance and spirit occurs and the prophecies of various cultures are the seeing of how spirit will manifest in a particular way as matter moves through time.

In ancient Greece there were two words for time, kairos and kronos. Kronos is quantitative, tick-tock, profane, temporal time. Kronos is birthdays, getting older, biological clocks, diaries, deadlines and appointments. We must adapt, time and tide will not wait. We have to immerse ourselves in life in order to get a life. We adapt to our collective reality and allow life to make its mark on us. Then, like the children of Kronos, we are eventually eaten by time.

Kairos, however, is sacred, eternal time. It is the right time, the moment of opportunity, the perfect time, the qualitative time, the "now." In the New Testament kairos means "the appointed time in the purpose of God." It is the time when God acts. It cannot be measured, only experienced. In these moments everything "flows" timelessly and without effort. Time stands still, an hour passes in a second, a second stretches to eternity. These moments occur when we draw close to the other world, often in archetypal situations of intense creativity, danger, ecstasy, lovemaking, or death. They transcend kronos and stir emotions and realisations that result in decisive action. "Carpe diem!"—Seize the day. Then we leave our mark on time itself. Kairos alters destiny and destiny alters kairos. To miss kronos is inconvenient. To miss kairos is tragedy.

Kairos is when our free will choice acts on what life offers us and diverts the stream of collective history or an individual life in unimaginable directions. Kairos moments (and the dates now become important) are those upon which personal or collective destiny turn. For example, Lincoln's two-minute Gettysburg address in November 1863 where he declared that "government of the people, by the people, for the people, shall not perish from the earth." Churchill's speech to the House of Commons in June 1940 when he said, "This was their finest hour." Kennedy's assassination on November 22, 1963. And 9/11.

Opportunity

Our twenties is the time of opportunity, the world is young and it's our oyster; we are not yet weighed down by the senex responsibilities of life. We are free to roam, to travel, to develop in any direction we want. The narrowing—of opportunities, of choices, of arteries—is yet to come.

So opportunity is part of our theme, one of the associative nodes that cluster around the notion of time and the passage of life. In Latin, the word portus means opening or passage through, as in a shipping port or the port (window) of a ship. Opportunus is that which offers or suggests an opening or a way through. The porta fenestrella was the opening through which Fortune passed. The Greek term for opportunity was kairos, one of the meanings of which was a "penetrable opening." Greek archers would practise by aiming at an opening, a kairos. We have seen that the moon is associated with weaving and in weaving the kairos is the opportune moment for the weaver to send the shuttle across the threads before the opening is closed.

There are two ends to the stick of opportunity—the presenting and the taking. Senex-like, Samuel Goldwyn said, "The harder I work, the luckier I get," as if the work ethic was all, and all luck was made by human hands. Indeed, we make our own luck but that is sales seminar simplification. Life, quite independently of our hard work and best intentions, offers us crisis or opportunity. But for life to present itself to us, we must be awake enough to notice. The more we notice life-as-it-presents-itself, the more life will present us with opportunities (irrespective of how hard we "work"). When the opportunus opens before us we must step through it.

"There is something you ought to be aware of by now," don Juan Matus said. "I call it the cubic centimetre of chance. Any of us, whether or not we are warriors, have a cubic centimetre of chance that pops out in front of our eyes from time to time. The difference between an average man and a warrior is that the warrior is aware of this, and one of his tasks is to be alert, deliberately waiting, so that when his cubic centimetre pops out he has the necessary speed, the prowess to pick it up."[21]

In ancient Greece the windfall, the stroke of luck, or lucky find, was a called a hermaion, a gift from Hermes. Opportunity is the dance between the propitious time that opens up a long window, the chance moment when something shouts briefly from the other world, our presence of mind to notice what falls in front of us, and the skill, daring, effort or endurance to pick up the hermaion. Knowing where we stand on the Moon Cycles increases our chances of catching our opportunities and being caught by our fate.

---

[21] Carlos Castaneda, *Journey to Ixtlan*, 234.

3

The Big Moons

To everything there is a season, a time to every purpose under heaven. —Ecclesiastes 3:1

God didn't want everything to happen all at once, so he invented time. —Anon.

The Moon Cycles are an aide-mémoire to the business of the soul and a reminder that "to everything there is a season." First, I will outline the Big and Little Moon Cycles and the Chaotic Journeys. The images and archetypes that stand behind them are the moon, the number 9, and the length of human pregnancy. Together they weave a pattern that shows us why age 27 is important. Regarding ages, the numerical notation is in years and months. For example: 27.3 is twenty-seven years and three months; 30.11 is thirty years and eleven months.

The Medicine Wheel

Everything the Power of the World does is done in a circle. The sky is round, and I have heard that the earth is round like a ball and so are all the stars. The wind, in its greatest power, whirls. Birds make their nests in circles, for theirs is the same religion as ours. The sun comes forth and goes down again in a circle. The moon does the same, and both are round. Even the seasons form a great circle in their changing.… The life of man is a circle from childhood to childhood, and so it is in everything where power moves.

—Black Elk

The medicine wheel is an archetypal image of wholeness. It occurs world-wide and time-wide in different forms although its form in the Americas is best known. The wisdom of the indigenous peoples of Turtle Island (North, South and Central America) has been distilled from inner and outer experience into a vast body of knowledge, at least as deep and as broad as the knowledge in our Western culture.

The medicine wheel is the basic pattern for understanding the influences of the Moon Cycles. Each direction on the wheel draws on the energies of the directions on either side of it. The cardinal directions hold or stabilise the wheel in the tonal (this physical world) and are compensatory to, and balance, each other. The non-cardinal directions spin or move the wheel in the nagual (the world of spirit) and are complementary to each other. Each cardinal direction has a non-cardinal on either side that compensates its stability, and each non-cardinal has a cardinal on either side that compensates its instability. To offer a fuller understanding of the medicine wheel is beyond the scope of this book, but we will amplify some of the meaning of the directions when we look at the Little Moons.

NORTH
ELEMENT: Air
COLOUR: White
WORLD: Animals
ASPECT: Mind
TEACHINGS: Wisdom and Knowledge, Receiving with Caring, Mental Flexibility
SHADOW: Philosophies and Beliefs

NORTHWEST
Laws, Cycles and Patterns, Book of Life

NORTHEAST
Design of Energy, Choices and Decisions

WEST
ELEMENT: Earth
COLOUR: Black
WORLD: Minerals
ASPECT: Body
TEACHINGS: Introspection and Intuition, Holding with Intimacy, Physical Stability
SHADOW:

EAST
ELEMENT: Fire
COLOUR: Yellow
WORLD: Humans
ASPECT: Spirit
TEACHINGS: Illumination and Enlightenment, Determining with Passion, Spiritual Expansiveness,
SHADOW: Fantasy and Illusion

CENTRE
Void, Catalyst Energy

N / NW / NE / W / E / SW / SE / S

SOUTHWEST
Symbols of Life Experience, Personal and Sacred Dream

SOUTH
ELEMENT: Water
COLOUR: Red
WORLD: Plants
ASPECT: Heart
TEACHINGS: Trust and Innocence, Giving with Tenderness, Emotional Fluidity
SHADOW: Mythology and Entertainment

SOUTHEAST
Self-Image, Ancestors

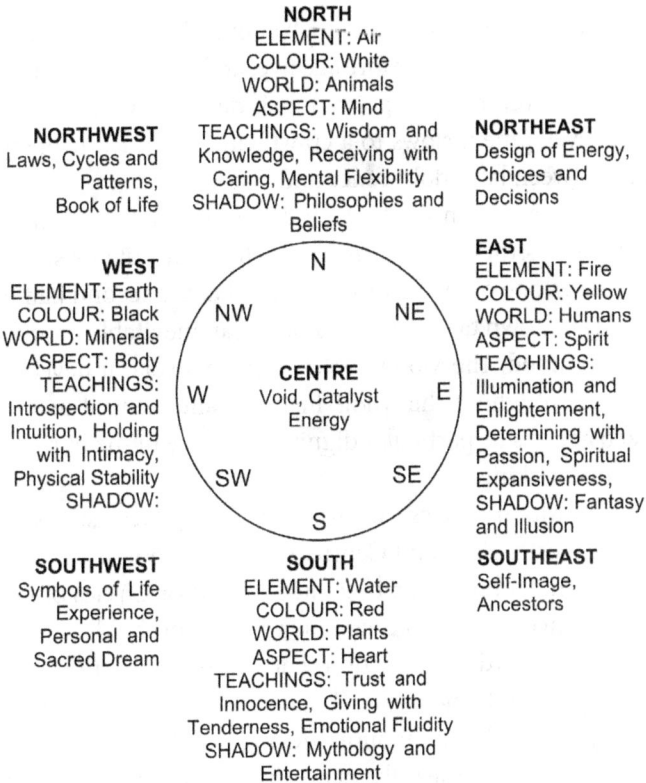

Figure 1: The Medicine Wheel

The Moon Cycles

The Moon Cycles tell us where we stand at a particular age in our movement around the Wheel of Life. We are influenced by different archetypal powers as we pass through each of the eight directions of the medicine wheel. The Moon Cycles help us understand what the archetypal climate is, and what challenges and opportunities are likely to face us, at a particular age.

Modern developmental psychology, with its cognitive, behavioural or biological orientation, has lots to say about child development but not much about adult development. Most of the action is before age five, and by the end of adolescence everything is pretty much developed. From then on, development slows to a crawl with not much happening between late adolescence and death.

However, when the body and the mind have run their course it is then that spiritual development hits its stride. Jung was one of the first to consider that the second half of life has its own tasks and was not just an inevitable product of childhood. The Moon Cycles offer a map of our development throughout the whole life span and remind us that each age has its particular dignity and place in the business of soul-making.

The Moon Cycles consist of five Big Moons: South, West, North, East, and Centre. Each Big Moon is 27 years in length, and made up of 9 Little Moons or Circles of Life Experience of 3 years each. Each Big Moon holds the energy of its cardinal direction. Each Little Moon holds the energy of both the cardinal and non-cardinal directions. Every four and a half months, during each Little Moon, our perspective, and the influences of the directions, shift as we move around each 3-year cycle.

We enter each Little Moon through the south— the place of innocence, not-knowing or unconsciousness— travel clockwise and exit through the east, the place of illumination or consciousness, having hopefully gained some life experience and learning. Note that we do not cross the southeast, instead we travel from the east of one Moon to the south of the next Moon and go through a 9-month Chaotic Journey. The exception to this is during the first 9 months after we are born.

We are born into the Little Centre Moon of the Big South Moon and, at age 27, leave childhood behind and

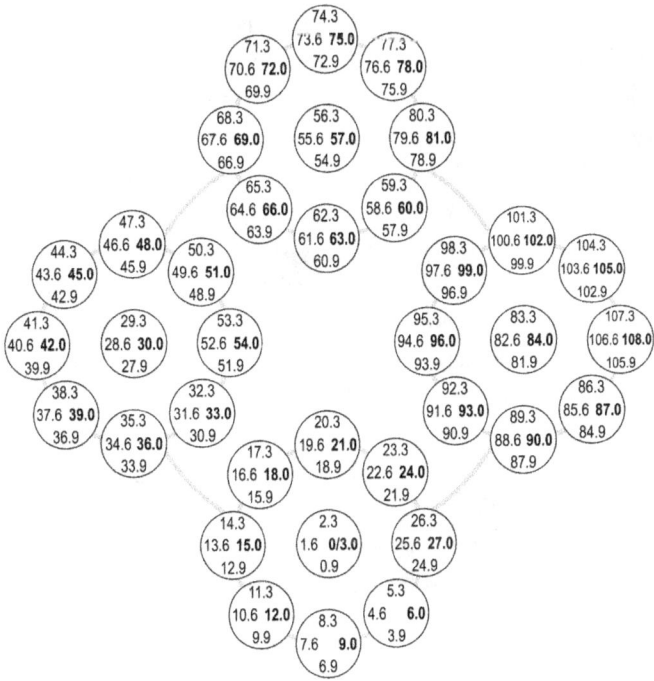

Figure 2: The Moon Cycles

move into the Big West Moon. At age 54 we move into the Big North; at age 81 into the Big East; and at age 108 into the Big Centre Moon. Each of the Big Moons carries the powers and gifts of its cardinal direction and during each 27 year cycle we are most influenced by, and able to receive, the teachings and gifts of that particular direction.

The name of each Moon (Child, Adolescent, Adult and Elder) refers to the maturation of the soul, which is a Moon Cycle (27 years) behind the socially recognised stage of physical or social maturation. In other words, we are a child until age 27, an adolescent until age 54, become an adult in our mid-fifties, and attain elderhood in our eighties.

Each 27-year Big Moon cycle is divided into 9 Little Moons each of 3 years' duration. There are eight Little Moons around the wheel and one in the centre. At any one time we are subject to the combined influences of three archetypal forces: The energy of the particular direction of the Little Moon we are in; the energy of the Little Moon itself; and the energy of the Big Moon. So, for example, on our 27th birthday we are in the east of the Little East Moon of the Big South Moon. Here, we are influenced by the energies of illumination and enlightenment (a double dose, as we are in the east of the Little East Moon) and trust and innocence. It is the last goodbye to childhood. The developmental imperative, conscious or unconscious, is to review our life since we were born and to grow up. We are confronted by the questions, "Who am I?" "Where have I come from?" and "Where am I going?"

0–27 Big South Moon

In each cardinal direction on the medicine wheel sits an element (water, earth, air, fire, and void in the centre) and an aspect of our humanness (heart, body, mind, spirit and soul) which are the guiding forces of the corresponding Big Moons.

In the Big South Moon we learn through trust and innocence with the heart. It is the time of learning trust in self, life, and others, through our relationships with those in our human family. Psychologists call this attachment. We learn emotionally through the element of water and the fluidity of the emotions. As children we learn to trust or mistrust our and other's emotions. Too much water and we drown, too little and we wither. We learn containment of our emotions, expression of our emotions, how to put them to work for us, which ones are too painful for us, and so on. But we all have sore spots, hurt places, childish places that we hide, and hide from. If we remain childish and linger too long in the Big South Moon then we will always be at the mercy of our moods and either hurt others or get hurt by others.

During this Big South Moon we also create our mythology, our identity, or self-concept. This is the conscious story of who we are or might become, as well as the ego's view of itself, its connection to the world around it, and its history and future. Mythology happens whenever we recognise a meaningful texture in seemingly coincidental outward facts, inner joys and sorrows, human encounters, and fateful patterns. The intellect views mythology as primitive fantasy but emotionally it is the story-that-heals and it gives life richness, eccentricity, and depth. One's personal mythology is the tapestry of a life that collective or scientific norms can only clumsily describe and it can only be adequately expressed in myth.

Throughout this Child Moon we develop our most comfortable place on the Wheel of Life. In the north in the place of thinking, concepts and ideas; in the south in the place of feeling, emotions and relationships; in the west in the place of sensation, the physical world and our body; or in the east, in the world of intuition, spirit and creativity. Whatever sits directly across the Wheel from our place of comfort (which Jung called our dominant or superior function) remains least developed and will press for recognition later in life in the Big West Moon. Jung called this our inferior function.

27–54 Big West Moon

> The psychological rule says that when an inner situa-
> tion is not made conscious, it happens outside as fate.
> —C G Jung

> After forty every man is responsible for his own face.
> —Abraham Lincoln

In the Child Moon everything is growing and possibilities
are endless. Western culture is a child culture. But in the
Adolescent Moon we now learn, not through trust and innocence with the emotions, but through death and change
experienced with the body. We have to come down to earth
and are forced, often unwillingly, to accept our limitations
and our strengths. The 27 Club members have all, each in
their own way, railed against this growing up and declared
their final and irreversible "No!"

Anything, either positive or negative, which has been
unresolved, buried, hidden, or ignored during the first 27
years, comes to the surface as part of the psyche's instinc-
tual drive for wholeness. This reaches its peak between 39
and 42 years of age in the Little West Moon of the Big West
Moon. Specifically, say the Moon Cycles, at age 40.6 in the
place of triple death and change. Yes, it's the "mid-life crisis" as it has come to be known, or come to be dismissed.
This is where we learn that death, physical or emotional, is
a part of life. It is the place of introspection, intuition and
looks-within. Here we learn primarily through action, the
body, and the element of earth. If we are not able to look
within and take responsibility for our own soul, we blame
others and life for our circumstances. If we linger in the
water consciousness of the Big South Moon past our time

we become the puer. If we do not meet life as death and change, then death—physical or spiritual—will meet us.

Erich Fromm, the social psychologist and psychoanalyst said, "The older such people get, the more that they cling to the illusion that one day they will do it. In certain people, the reaching of a certain age, generally at the beginning of the forties, brings a sobering effect so that they then begin to use their own forces, or there is a neurotic breakdown."

54–81 Big North Moon

This is the time of learning through harmony and balance with the mind. This Moon teaches Wisdom and Logic; not the logic of the intellect, but the logic of the universe. It is what the Stoics called the logos spermatikos, the fertilising voice of the Holy Spirit. It is also the understanding of the inner laws of the Self which allow us freedoms and impose restrictions that are our own unique fate. On the shadow side, if we remain in the earth Moon of the West too long, we become unable to receive new knowledge, unable to look at things from a different viewing point on the wheel, and our philosophies and beliefs become fanatical, rigid, grumpy and stagnant. We become the negative senex or seneca. On the light side, this is the place of the sage or crone, the wise man or wise woman, who has married both thinking and feeling and birthed wisdom.

81–108 Big East Moon

At the age of eighty-one we enter the Big East Moon, the Big Moon of illumination and enlightenment. The age of eighty-one represents consciousness of pattern (pattern 8 + 1 consciousness = 9 movement), and is 9 cycles of 9 (9 x 9 = 81). Here we learn through the illumination of spirit as we look backwards on our life, our earthwalk, and look forwards to our death and the journey to the beach of stars. If we remain with the air of the north too long, we are unable to touch the light and warmth of spirit in the east, and we fall back into the shadow side of the south in childish nostalgia, or into the west in fear of the barren coldness of physical death.

4

The Chaotic Journeys

Chaos often breeds life, when order breeds habit.
—Henry Adams

In all chaos there is a cosmos, in all disorder a secret order. —C. G. Jung

Rhythm and pattern are born from formlessness. Life sucks order from a sea of disorder. Order and chaos are not the best of friends and, like jealous sisters or hostile brothers, they have an uneasy peace. The original chaos is the Void where space is so infinite that it has no meaning, and time, by which the formation and destruction of all things is measured, is not yet born.

The Void is the mother of all things, the dark within the light. The very darkness of her womb yearns for insemination, to see within herself her lover and her opposite. So chaos births order, the light within the dark, the father of all things. We live between order and chaos. To become what we will, we must return, after times of order and structure, to the dark ground of chaos where there is no rhythm or pattern. It is the cosmic eraser, the reset button, which exposes us to chance.

Every 3 years, we arrive in the east of a Little Moon. Instead of continuing our journey around the wheel through the southeast, we travel through 9 months of chaos to arrive in the south of the next Little Moon. For the first month of this Chaotic Journey we stand in the light of consciousness of the east and look back over the last 3 years, or in the case of the Big Moons, the last 27 years.

The Chaotic Journey is so called because we are between Moons and no longer subject to the archetypal patterning of those Moons. Eighty percent of all movement of energy in the universe is patterned, and twenty percent is the free will of the Creator, or the laws of chance. Because this will is unknown and unknowable, it appears to us as chaos and the Chaotic Journey is often a time of disorientation and confusion when we are outside of pattern.

First Big Chaotic Journey

The journey between the Big Moons is called the Big Chaotic Journey (27.0 to 27.9; 54.0 to 54.9; 81.0 to 81.9) and, between the Little Moons, the Little Chaotic Journey. Because the Chaotic Journeys are outside of pattern, and are an "in-between" time, the events that occur during a Chaotic Journey can be considered as belonging to either the Moon that comes before, or the Moon that comes after, or to both.

All the Chaotic Journeys are internal journeys. The only time we cross the southeast externally is during the first Little Moon after we are born. We are born into the east of the Little Centre Moon and travel clockwise through the southeast at 4½ months, into the south at 9 months, the west at 18 months, the north at 27 months and arrive in the east again at age 3.

These first 9 months of life are critically important as a prototype for later Chaotic Journeys in our lives (how we cope with chaos, change, trauma, confusion) and in all the Little Southeast Moons (how we see ourselves, our self-image, our "self-esteem"). The reason for this is that although the baby is physically born in the east of the Little Centre Moon, it is not psychologically born until it is in the south of that Moon, and the first 9 months of life is the journey in the outside womb after 9 months in the inside womb.

At age 27 we take our first Big Chaotic Journey from the east of the Little East Moon of the Big South Moon (the Child Moon of trust and innocence) to the south of the Little Centre Moon of the Big West Moon (the Adolescent Moon of death and change). This Chaotic Journey is the first we undertake after we are born and it occupies almost the whole year after we turn 27.

The first month of this Chaotic Journey is a time to look back, in the light of the east, at the teachings of the previous 27 years. At the end of our Chaotic Journey we arrive at south of the Little Centre Moon of the Big West and travel clockwise around this Little Centre Moon until age 30. We then go on a Little Chaotic Journey and arrive in the south of the Little Southeast Moon at the age of 30 years 9 months.

This pattern is repeated 9 times until we leave the Big West Moon at age 54 years. At each Little Moon, we enter in the south and leave in the east. At each Big Moon we enter in the south of the Little Centre Moon and leave from the east of the Little East Moon.

At age 54 we take our second Big Chaotic Journey from the Big West Moon to the Big North Moon (the Adult Moon of wisdom and knowledge). This second journey can also be a perilous time or a transition with great reward. All things that have remained unresolved from the last Chaotic Journey at age 27 will surface again for the purpose of resolution at age 54.

After his initial successes as an actor James Dean took up auto racing. During the filming of *Rebel Without a Cause* he bought a Porsche 550 Spyder which he was driving when he was killed in 1955 at age 24. Dean's passenger was Rolf Wütherich, his German mechanic. Wütherich, himself badly injured in the crash, received hate mail for the rest of his life from Dean fans who blamed him for the actor's death.

Wütherich was born August 5, 1927 and the accident in which Dean was killed happened when he was 28 years, 3 months and 25 days old. He survived numerous dangerous car crashes during his lifetime as well as attempting suicide several times. On July 22, 1981 he died in a car crash in the town centre of Kupferzell, Germany. Whilst intoxicated he drove his Honda Civic into an office building. Wütherich was 53 years, 11 months and 17 days old and about to go on his second Big Chaotic Journey.

5

The Little Moons

When innocence has been deprived of its entitlement it becomes a diabolical spirit. —James Grotstein

Only absolute totality can renew itself out of itself and generate itself anew. —C. G. Jung

To understand what happens at age 27 we must look at what happens in the first twenty-seven years of life during the Little Moons of the Big South Maoon.

0–3 Catalyst of Childhood

The centre is the place of the Void, the nothingness from which all things are born and to which all things return. It produces change without itself being changed, it unites the opposites, and makes the wheel turn without itself turning.

These Little Centre Moons are the ones that catalyse or set the trajectory for the next Big Moon. They are from ages 0–3, 27–30, 54–57, 81–84 years and are the Moons of the catalyst energy—love and sexuality. This is where what we do, or what is done to us, has a profound impact on the course of the next 27 year cycle.

The Little Centre Moon of the Big South Moon (0–3 years) is the catalyst of childhood. It is the critical period for learning about the catalyst energy, love. It is the story of attachment to Life itself, the positive, nurturing aspect of the Great Mother, as mediated through the personal mother.

In contrast, the Little Centre Moon of the Big West (27–30) is the story is of attachment to death and change, the power of Life as the Death-Mother, and the capacity to destroy in the service of creation, as mediated through our intimate adult relationships.

In the sense that individuation (becoming the unique person that we are) is an opus contra naturam (a work against nature), we begin to fashion a life out of what life has given us. As the years from birth to 3 are about the beginnings of the child personality and knowing trust and innocence (or its violation) and the years from 27 to 30 are about bedding-in the adult personality and realising we have both a positive and negative shadow.

In the Big West, now that one Big Moon Cycle has been completed, the Little Moons begin to resonate with similar experiences in the past, in the same moons, and opposite moons across the wheel, of the Big South Moon. If there is trauma, neglect, hurt or pain in the first 3 years of life, these will return again, in perhaps a different form, in the next Little Centre Moon from age 27–30.

3–6 Self-Image of Childhood

The Little Southeast Moons are from ages 3–6, 30–33, 57–60 and 84–87 years. They are the place where the ego's image of itself is formed. The ego is what we commonly refer

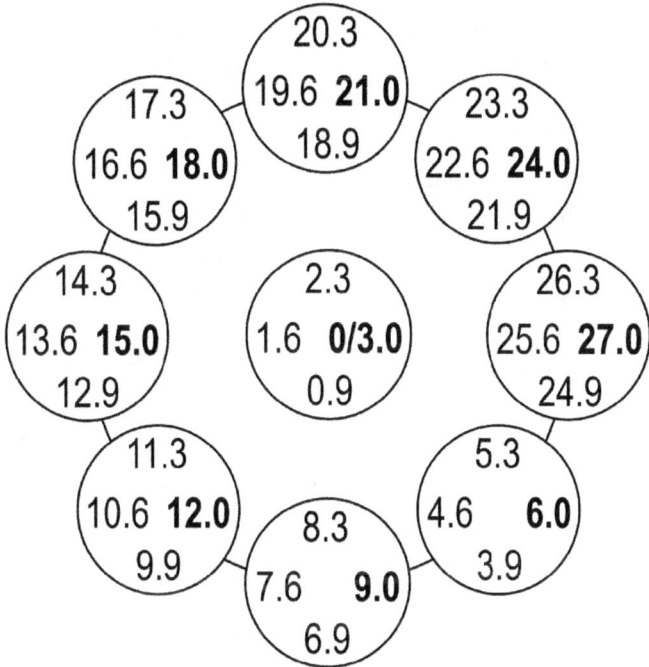

Figure 3: The Little Moons of the Big South Moon

to when we say "I." It is what we are consciously aware of in ourselves.

We have seen that from 0–3 years the groundwork is laid for the development of the personality. In the Little Southeast Moon from 3–6 years of age the distinct personality of the child (the "me," the self-image) emerges. This repeats itself in the Little Southeast Moon of the Big West Moon from 30–33 years when the adult personality emerges.

But there is more to us than our conscious minds are aware of. The problem is that the ego doesn't know this and can get out of balance with the whole personality. If the ego thinks we are smaller than we are then we have the ubiquitous "low self-esteem." If the ego gets up itself and too big for its boots then we have arrogance, narcissism and grandiosity. Grandiosity is the occupational hazard of rock stardom. For those who are vulnerable to puffing-up, who identify with what they portray on stage, the screams of the fans, or the marketing hype, they will eventually implode psychologically and the opposites of grandiosity—depression, self-hatred, emotional turmoil and escalating drug use—will emerge.

6–9 Mythology of Childhood

Little South Moons occupy the years 6–9, 33–36, 60–63 and 84–87. The Little South Moon of the Big South Moon (6–9 years) are the years of double south, that is, the years of double trust and innocence, the quintessence of childhood. Age 6.9 is the south of the Little South Moon of Big South Moon, the place of triple trust and innocence.

The south is the place of trust and innocence, the element of water, the colour red, the plants, and the number 3. It is the place of the trinity, growth and sacrifice. The number 3 is associated with the creative process. Dynamic, developmental and temporal processes are often configured in 3s: a beginning, middle and end; past, present and future. Deities are often images of threeness, for example, the Father (Self), the Son (ego), and the Holy Ghost (ego and Self); or the triple goddess, maiden, mother, and crone, the ones who hold the feminine cycles of life, the 3 times 3, the 9, the pregnancy.

The water in the south is symbolic of washing, purification, rejuvenation, new beginnings, amniotic fluid, emotional fluidity, and the alchemical solutio. In medieval alchemy the first step of "The Work" was solutio or dissolving. The alchemists thought of this as a return to the womb for the purpose of rebirth, and that no change could come about until everything had been reduced to the prima materia (the first matter). The south is where we start to go around the wheel, the place of the child, beginnings, futurity, and hope. So these years are the childhood of each of the Big Moons where we are both blessed and wounded by our own innocence, and some of this innocence must be sacrificed for life to move on.

9–12 Dream of Childhood

The Little Southwest Moons are the years 9–12, 36–39, 63–66 and 87–90 and the place of the symbols of life experience. It is the time of longing, dreaming, imagining and yearning. Jung said, "Psychic development cannot be accomplished by intention and will alone; it needs the attraction of symbol, whose value quantum exceeds that of the cause." This means that movement in our lives cannot be brought about solely by willpower and pushing ourselves. We must also be drawn into the future by the power of something that is not yet known to us. This is best represented by a symbol.

12–15 Death of Childhood

The Little West Moons occur at 12–15, 39–42, 66–69 and 90–93 years of age. The west is the place of death and change, the colour black, the body, and the place of the woman as life-giver (ovulation) and death-bringer (menstruation). In each West Moon what already exists is destroyed in order to create new life. In adolescence, with the coming of the sun (ejaculation) and the coming of the moon (menstruation), the physical body changes; at mid-life the body of our lives (work, family, home, relationships) changes; in the late sixties the mental body changes (beliefs about life and death). In these Little West Moons, we have 3 major life transitions: adolescence, mid-life, and retirement or the beginning of old age.

This Little West Moon of the Big South Moon (12–15 years) is the death and change of trust and innocence, of childhood, and the birth of intimacy with the body. Most notably, at age 13.6 we enter the west of the Little West Moon of the Big South Moon, the double death and change of trust and innocence. It is the birth of the teenager and the death of the child. JM Barrie, the author of Peter Pan and a puer himself, said, "Nothing that happens after we are twelve matters very much."

The symbolism of the number 13 is significant here. The number 12 has been considered a perfect number, whereas 13 indicates the beginning of a new cycle and so is a symbol of death and rebirth: the thirteen at the Last Supper led to Christ's betrayal and crucifixion; the thirteenth card of the tarot is the Death card; the Mayan Calendar cycle of 52 years made up of 4 x 13 year cycles; the thirteenth chapter of the Book of Revelation describes the Anti-Christ; and Odysseus, as the thirteenth member of his crew, escaped being eaten by the Cyclops.

At this age the psychological need for initiation is strong. The teen must mark the passage out of childhood in some way but the old religious markers like confirmation or Bar Mitzvah have lost their power. In Western sibling society all that is left is a messy self-initiation through the peer group. At best, this is ineffective in producing durable psychological change and a change in recognised social status. At worst, it results in death through a car accident or an overdose.

The west of the next two Little West Moons occurs at 40.6 and 67.6. Age 40.6 is the time of triple Death and Change (west of the Little West Moon of the Big West Moon) and is the dead centre of mid-life.

Two literary examples: Jack London (January 12, 1876 – November 22, 1916, 40 years 10 months 10 days). London was an American author, journalist, and social activist. He wrote *Call of the Wild* and *White Fang* and died from kidney failure and chronic alcoholism.

Edgar Allan Poe (January 19, 1809 – October 7, 1849, 40 years 8 months 19 days). Poet and author of *The Black Cat*, *The Fall of the House of Usher* and *The Murders in the Rue Morgue*. The cause of his death was undetermined and has been variously attributed to alcoholism, drugs, heart disease, suicide, and tuberculosis.

Age 67.6 is the double death and change of wisdom and knowledge and another risk period for death or suicide. In the eighteen months following retirement at 65 the mortality rate from heart disease increases.

Gonzo journalist Hunter Thompson (July 18, 1937 – February 20, 2005, 67 years 7 months 2 days) shot himself. Author of *Fear and Loathing in Las Vegas* and a lifestyle of guns, drugs, and drink. His suicide note read: "No More Games. No More Bombs. No More Walking. No More Fun. No More Swimming. 67. That is 17 years past 50. 17 More than I needed or wanted. Boring. I am always bitchy. No Fun—for anybody. You are getting Greedy. Act your old age. Relax—this won't hurt."

Lucy Maud Montgomery (November 30, 1874 – April 24, 1942, 67 years 4 months 25 days). Author of *Anne of Green Gables*, committed suicide by drug overdose.[22]

---

[22] The Heartbreaking Truth About Anne's Creator. http://v1.theglobeandmail.com/servlet/story/RTGAM.20080919.wmhmontgomery0920/BNStory/mentalhealth/

Primo Levi, the Jewish-Italian scientist and writer, who had spent a year in Auschwitz when he was 25, jumped to his death from the third floor interior balcony of his apartment building. He was 67 years and 8 months old. Author Elie Wiesel said at the time: "Primo Levi died at Auschwitz forty years earlier."

15–18 Rules and Laws of Childhood

The Little Northwest Moons (15–18, 42–45, 69–72, 93–96 years) are where we confront laws, patterns and cycles—personal, social and universal. In the Little Northwest Moon of the Big South, between the ages of 15 and 18, we encounter them in the form of the secular laws of our family, peer group, religion, or culture. At 16, we can drive a car. At 18, in the east of the Little Northwest Moon—the place of the illumination and enlightenment of laws and patterns—we are considered mature enough to vote.

At ages 42–45 and 69–72, we encounter not external rules but the internal laws or "morality" of the Self. Jung said, "Just as our free will clashes with necessity in the outside world, so also it finds its limits outside the field of consciousness in the subjective inner world, where it comes into conflict with the facts of the self."

These Moons are often a time of moral dilemmas in deciding which strivings and impulses, some of which may fly in the face of convention, are ones that we should act on or suppress. Responsibility for this decision rests with the ego, which must decide which parts of the shadow it lives out, or with. This brings about a crucifixion. The morality of the Self may or may not coincide with the prevailing social morality, and so places a much greater burden on us individually. We have to be honest to live outside the law. But this does not mean a complete rejection of collective values and norms. Jung said that the only valid reason for going outside the boundaries and conventions of one's culture or group was if, in doing so, one brought back something of greater value to the collective.

18–21 Wisdom of Childhood

> Since I have not the gift of belief, I only can say whether I know something or not.… A belief proves to me only the phenomenon of belief, not the content of the belief. —C. G. Jung

The Little North Moons (18–21, 45–48, 72–75, 96–99 years) are the moons of wisdom and knowledge and their shadow, philosophies and beliefs. The south is the place of experience whereas the north is the place of making meaning out of that experience. The north teaches us mental flexibility and imagination, inter-connectedness, discrimination, and receiving with the mind.

The Little North Moon of the Big South, from the age of 18 to 21, is the time we look across the wheel of life into our mythology in the south, and develop our philosophies and beliefs about the meaning of life. It is a time of learning knowledge and receiving with the mind. We choose a job, career or profession within which to gain knowledge. We look to role models, mentors, elders and guides to assimilate those qualities and knowledges that fill out our image of who we are and who we want to become.

This happens again at a different level from ages 45–48 and again from 72–75. The north is the place of being able to see from multiple viewpoints, from all points around the medicine wheel. The shadow side of the north is closed-mindedness and mental rigidity where the world is seen in terms of unalterable, opposing dualities. If we are mentally inflexible we are unable to receive new knowledge, unable to act without beliefs, and become a senex-like slave to our own opinions and their attendant emotions.

21–24 Choices of Childhood

> Man was created for the sake of choice.
>
> —Hebrew saying

The Little Northeast Moons (21–24, 48–51, 75–78, 99–102) are the moons of choices and decisions—deciding how we want to use our life energy (money, time, inspiration, ideas, sex, love, the car). The northeast is the place where we direct our use of energy around the rest of the wheel through the decisions we make. The Little Northeast Moon (21–24 years) is where begin to make more discriminating choices about where we want our life to go.

The first 27 years of life are spent getting a life, an ego and a personality. We find ways to become a useful human being and have begun to take a place in our community. This is the result of a myriad of choices—some are our own, some we think are our own but are really the cultural or family values that we kick against or embrace, and sometimes life just chooses for us.

All this relentless choosing during adolescence (the first time we get control over our choices) and our twenties force us down an ever-narrowing path. By choosing we also refuse. There is always the road not taken, the could-have-been, the almost, the one that got away. In the stir and rush of life these roads not taken recede quickly behind us but in our late twenties the consequences of our choices come to a head. We are now defined, we've been there done that, have a trade or career, have a relationship, have children, have a mortgage, have a house, have dreams. But equally we are caught, trapped, tied down, unable to tie the knot, are "afraid of commitment" as they say, and generally kick against anything that narrows our possibilities, takes away our precious "freedom of choice." For the puer, all decisions once made must remain open, with a secret escape hatch, because deciding means the final loss of the road that was maybe still available, and every decision leads us closer to the grave.

24–27 Illumination of Childhood

The Little East Moons (24–27, 51–54, 78–81, 105–108 years) are the moons of illumination and enlightenment. At the end of each Little East Moon, at ages 27, 54 and 81 we sit in the east of the east—the place of double illumination.

In this Little East Moon from 24 to 27, the last moon of the Big South, we take stock of our adolescence and our twenties and begin to feel like an adult. It is a time of learning about consciousness and determining the direction of our life with our own fire, our spirit. Throughout the twenties, the tension increases between the self-image we borrow from the culture (the Little Northeast Moon) or our heroes and mentors (the Little North Moon), and the direction indicated by our own spirit.

This is a time of when, wittingly or not, we review what has happened to us in the past 3 years or the past 27 years and where we are going in our lives.[23] It is here that we ac-

---

[23] For example see thoughtcatalog.com/jinky-grace-nono/2017/04/16-thoughts-ive-learned-about-life-at-age-27/ and www.huffingtonpost.com/natacha-hildebrand/twenty-seven_b_3645803

tualise the consciousness gained on our journey around the wheel. If there has been no broadening of consciousness, or if we allow what has been gained to sink back into the unconscious, then the next Moon Cycle will present us again with what is unresolved.

The lightning bolt of illumination—the Ah-hah!, the sudden glimpse of what has been in the darkness of the unconscious, of what we have been unaware of—is characteristic of the east. If we are able to claim for ourselves some consciousness, some illumination and enlightenment, we are able to move on. If we cling to the remnants of childishness, the powers of death and change are increasingly constellated.

The light is the place where the darkness is clearest. These two great powers are most in opposition in the east of the Little East Moons or the west of the Little West Moons. At 27, most of us look more grown up on the outside than we feel on the inside. Sometimes we feel like an imposter, faking it, not quite up to the job, so we put on the right face. Often when a rock star suicides or dies under questionable circumstances there are reports like, "No, no, he wasn't depressed! In fact, just a few days before he [committed suicide] he was telling me what great plans he had for the future."

The light constellates the dark, the dark constellates the light. Clinicians know that in springtime there is an increase in suicides. They know that the riskiest time for suicide is not in the depths of depression but when a person is coming up out of the hole and seeing the light.

For those who are creative, who have been touched by fire, this last moon of childhood is a crossroads between light and dark and is crucial in whether, and how, they continue their journey. The result of resisting the movement into the Big West Moon and the next 27 years of death and change, is the psychology of the puer. Or to put it another way, the puer resists moving into the Big West. Many creative young men and women are secretly identified with the other world, experiencing this world as a pale, disappointing imitation. This closeness with the collective unconscious, with the world of fire and spirit and creativity, is both the wisdom and the folly of the young person. It can lead to a lack of adaptation to life, often with a touch of genius, which sometimes results in early death.

More commonly, as the puer grows into middle age, he dies an emotional or spiritual death, rather than a physical death. His emotional life remains at an adolescent level and he typically lives a provisional life, does not want to be committed or tied down, bucks at boundaries and limitations, and is always over- or under-reaching himself. What he has is never quite right and he is often full of big plans that are about to hatch but nothing happens.

As he moves out of late middle age (often around the mid-fifties in the transition from the Big West to the Big North Moon) the puer increasingly becomes his shadow— the curmudgeon, the rule-bound, grumpy old man who is impossible to please. The puer becomes what he hated a Big Moon Cycle earlier.

Nothing left to do but run, run, run

> Not to touch the earth
> Not to see the sun
> Nothing left to do, but
> Run, run, run
> Let's run
>   —The Doors, *Waiting for the Sun*, 1968

On the medicine wheel the north is the place where we receive wisdom and knowledge through the mind and gain
the perspective necessary to see things from 360 degrees
around the wheel. It is in the Little North Moon from 18–21
that we begin to see our gifts and our wounds. At that age
we get an education—that is, we capitalise on what we have
learned we are good at, or at least what others have told us
we are good at. From 21–24 we make decisions based on
this learning and from 24–27 we sit in the light of the Little
East Moon, the golden age and pinnacle of physical youth.

We produce our physical best in our early- to mid-twenties, when for example, the best sprint or middle distance
performances begin to show. Modern medical knowledge
extends this period into the late twenties but it is rare to
find an Olympic medallist over the 100 to 800 metre events
(or even 1500 metres) who is over 30. Regarding our cognitive best, it seems that our memory and speed of cognitive
processing is at its peak at around age 22 and that age-related decline begins about age 27.[24]

Although I focus in this book on the shadow side of 27
there is an equally important light side. But this 27 Club
hardly shows on the news radar. The Little East Moon from
24–27 is a time of review and in the northeast of that moon
at about 26.6 we make decisions that change the trajectory
of our lives toward a destructive, negative path, or a life-af-
firming, positive path. Decisions made at that time may not
be conscious and only in retrospect do we sense that something deeper within in us was preparing for a shift. Then,
the Chaotic Journey beginning at 27.0 allows a 9-month
period of chaos, renewal and clearing the decks for the next
Big Moon.

---

[24] Salthouse, Timothy A. 2009. 'When Does Age-Related Cognitive Decline Begin?' *Neurobiology of Aging* 30 (4): 507–14.
https://doi.org/10.1016/j.neurobiolaging.2008.09.023.

Mo (Mohammed) Farah is a good example of a positive shift around age 27. Farah was born on March 23, 1983 in Mogadishu, Somalia and raised in Djibouti. He moved to the UK when he was eight years old and had to learn to speak English. An early junior success, he ran the second fastest 3,000 metres ever by a 14-year-old. He was there or thereabouts at world class level for many years but by his mid-twenties he had plateaued. He failed to reach the finals at the 2004 Athens and 2008 Beijing Olympics.

In late 2008 he spent four months training at altitude in Kenya (25 years 6 months, west of the Little East Moon of the Big South Moon, the illumination of the Death and Change of Childhood). "Kenya was different, it opened my eyes," explained Farah. "How they train is completely different. You wake up in the morning at 6 am and you've got loads of guys to run with. I turned up at the track at 8.30 am on the first morning and there was 50 guys or more just doing a track session." [25]

He would rise at 6 am and ten minutes later be out the door for a one-hour run. Afterwards he would eat breakfast often followed by a one-hour nap. Later he might have a gym session then lunch, a further sleep, and a second run of the day before sunset. He even trained twice on Christmas Day. "Run, eat, sleep, that's all I did."

In July 2010 (aged 27 years 4 months) he won both the 5,000 and 10,000 at the European Championships, his first major championship titles. In August 2010 he set a UK 5,000 metre record breaking David Moorcroft's 28-year-old record and becoming the first ever British athlete to run this distance in under 13 minutes.

---

[25] www.spikesmag.com/features/mofarahonhisafricantrain-ingtrip.aspx

In January 2011 (age 27 years 10 months), he separated from his long-time coach Alan Storey and moved his family from London to Eugene, Oregon. He began training with his new coach, consecutive three-time New York marathon winner and former American 5,000 and 10,000 metre record holder, Alberto Salazar.

In August 2011 he made a major breakthrough at the World Championships in South Korea by taking silver in the 10,000 and gold in the 5,000. After his World Championship successes he said of moving to Eugene, "I thought about it last year and the year before that [at age 26 and 27] but things weren't quite right and everything has seemed to come together now."

Now Sir Mo Farah (he was knighted in 2017), he won the 5,000 and 10,000 metres gold medals at the 2013 and 2015 World Championships and at the 2012 Olympics in London and 2016 Olympics in Rio de Janeiro.

6

The Science

I used to think that the brain was the most wonderful organ in my body. Then I realised who was telling me this. —Emo Phillips

In Dante's *Divine Comedy*, the gates of hell bear an inscription, the ninth (and final) line of which is the famous phrase, "Abandon all hope, ye who enter here." Those who lust for proof are likely to be cross-addicted to number and precision. For the scientifically-minded reader who is looking for what they define as proof (or refutation) of the existence of the 27 Club, I suggest they unclench or read elsewhere. To paraphrase Dante we might say, "Abandon all proof, ye who enter here."

Precision and proof

The alchemy of events that lead someone to join the 27 Club are complex and ultimately its threads are beyond counting. Those who value the precision of dates will be disappointed. If someone dies at age 26.11 and someone else dies two months later at 27.1, then it matters not from the point of view of the Moon Cycles. The pattern is what counts, not the data point. From a distance, I can tell if something is a tree or a cow without having to press for unnecessary correctness as to the breed or the species. So it is with the Moon Cycles and the personality constellation of the puer. If we defocus and do not insist on too much accuracy then the Moon Cycles become a map rather than a clock, and the puer becomes a pattern rather than a personality disorder.

Science values precision, peer review, accuracy, clarity, transparency, vision, edges, boundaries, definition, sharpness, reason, judgement, discrimination, objectivity, structure, and abstraction. It abhors all things vague, ambiguous, amorphous, blurred, dim, faint, fuzzy, hazy, ill-defined, imprecise, indefinite, indeterminate, indistinct, muddy, nebulous, obscure, occult, shadowy, tenebrous, uncertain or unclear. Whew! Robert Graves paints the difference between the two ways of seeing in his poem *Broken Images*.

He is quick, thinking in clear images;
I am slow, thinking in broken images.
He becomes dull, trusting to his clear images;
I become sharp, mistrusting in my broken images.
Trusting his images, he assumes their relevance;
Mistrusting my images, I question their relevance.
Assuming their relevance, he assumes the fact;
Questioning their relevance, I question the fact.
When the fact fails him, he questions his sense;
When the fact fails me, I approve my senses.
He continues quick and dull in his clear images;
I continue slow and sharp in my broken images.
He in a new confusion of his understanding;
I in a new understanding of my confusion.

Science and rationality specialise in a certain kind of consciousness that admits little else. They assume that the pinnacle of human achievement is the intellect and that we are or should be "rational" beings. But if people were "rational" then we would not continue to engage in an enterprise, like marriage for example, where there is a 40% "failure" rate. The evidence suggests that something other than rational choice is at work in the human psyche.

Jung said that we have four functions or ways of perceiving the world. Sensation is perception through the five senses. Intuition is perception through the sixth sense or the unconscious. These two functions simply register information; they tell us if something exists or not. Thinking is objective judgement, discrimination and sorting through measurement by external values—the collective laws or standards of the group or culture. Feeling is subjective judgement, discrimination and sorting through measurement by internal values or standards—our unique, personal taste. These two functions take the raw data of sensation and intuition and evaluate it. Thinking tells you what something is; it names the object. Feeling tells you whether you like it or not. The word *ratio* in Latin means "to calculate." Both thinking and feeling are rational in that they measure, but feeling measures with our personal ruler, while thinking measures with the social or scientific ruler.

What science calls superstition is, in its natural form, the psychological function of intuition. This consciousness is able to perceive connections between things that are not visible to the other five senses. This was taken for granted in indigenous cultures where the worlds of spirit and matter were in good relation. The aberration that was medieval Europe became estranged from its indigenous roots and the interconnectedness of all things became debased and concretised. So the black cat that crossed your path was the Devil's familiar and always brought bad luck; you always walked around the ladder not under it; the mole under the wise woman's armpit was always the mark of the Devil, and so on.

A psyche or a culture will attempt to right itself when it becomes too lopsided. Adam Smith, he of *The Inquiry into the Nature and Causes of the Wealth of Nations,* said "Science is the great antidote to the poison of enthusiasm and superstition." The clarifying vision of the Age of Enlightenment arose as compensation for the one-sidedness of the Middle Ages.

Science, then, was born from lopsidedness. Notwithstanding its great benefits, it has itself now become lopsided. The uses of the scientific and statistical net are limited— they catch the fish but not the water. More dangerously, science is unaware of its limitations. The pendulum has swung the other way and science now has the polar opposite belief to superstition. Now nothing is connected to anything else, nothing resonates with any other thing, and all connections must be proven by experiment and statistical association in order to be valid. Thus science often "discovers" the obvious. Life, however, does not consult the scientific literature before it proceeds.

The split between spirit and matter that occurred historically in Western culture has resulted in distortions and exaggerations of both science and intuition, the rational and the irrational. Distorted and exaggerated intuition becomes superstition, which sees too much connection between things. As a result paranoia and conspiracy theories multiply and we see profound connection, significance, meaning and mystery where there is none, particularly when a powerful archetype is activated (as when John F. Kennedy's assassination or 9/11 activated the death archetype) then the whole web, everything, not just the matter at hand, is pulled up from the collective unconscious. There is no discrimination afforded by either objective thinking or by subjective feeling, and everything is spookily connected. It is worth noting that much of the current conspiracy-deep state writing is authored by sensation-thinking types who gravitate toward science or have a scientific background but who have been captured by their inferior intuitive-feeling function.

Distortions and exaggerations of science on the other hand allow for no connections between things. Consequently, an association that is intuitively obvious is dismissed as not being a "fact" and is not permitted as evidence. In science, all is unproven until researched, more research is always needed, and movement is dull and plodding. Mark Twain said, "You can't rely on your judgement when your imagination is out of focus." Science has an imagination deficiency disorder. It's an objective net that is dumb and dense about feeling-tone, colour, taste, myth, beauty and all those subjective and immeasurable qualities that are food for the soul.

We don't elect our politicians on the basis of scientific research. The democratic process, for good or for ill, is based on the untidy warmth of subjective feeling, not on the neat coolness of objective thinking. And we don't do double-blind randomised, controlled trials to decide whom to fall in love or lust with. Or carry out a small statistical study on a subset of Renaissance masters to find out if the Mona Lisa is the most beautiful painting. Or ask a computer program to pick out which brush strokes produced the horror in Edvard Munch's "Scream."

The notion of the 27 Club has an intuitive-feeling validity that will not show up in the catch-net of thinking-sensation scientific research and has no need to be judged by those standards. The 27 Club points to something, some-where, sometime, in some way. The challenge is to bring it down from an intuitive notion and clothe it decently in observation, fact and feeling such that it can be shown into the polite company of the dominant sensation-thinking culture. This book's take on age 27 is that it is more like a road sign or a reminder to stay awake rather than an irra-tional silliness or a fated danger.

The prevalent attitudes toward the 27 Club are either the cynical ridicule and unthinking disbelief of science, or the naive acceptance and unthinking belief of superstition. In the first instance, it is dismissed as confirmation bias, ir-rational nonsense, statistical ignorance or tabloid fantasy. In the second, it is accepted uncritically as a curse. Neither position leads to greater consciousness.

The rational position is dominant at this time in history but the lie is given to its rationality by the degree of hysteria and emotionality shown by debunkers as, for example, the books on evolution by Richard Dawkins, "Darwin's Rott-weiler," former Oxford Professor of the Public Understand-ing of Science, or websites such as "The Reason Stick."[26] The men doth protest too much, methinks.

Most supposedly scientific reasoning about the 27 Club does not live up to its own evidence-based standards. Its notions about superstition are themselves superstitious. For example, the following is taken from an online article explaining the 27 Club as confirmation bias (my comments in brackets):

---

[26] www.crispian-jago.blogspot.com. "The Reason Stick: A blunt, shit-stained instrument wielded indiscriminately to bludgeon pseudoscience, superstition, blind faith and common or garden irrational bollocks."

There is a social psychology phenomenon known as causal attribution [OK, so we have named something but can you stroke it or eat it?]. This is when a person or society [or science] attributes outcomes to particular causes. When there is a tragic young death of a famous person, we tend to look for some reason why it happened [evidence, please], or in this case, why these deaths collectively happened. We try to make sense of it [evidence for this?]. And when we can't make sense of it, we find a way for it to make sense [evidence for this?]. So the "27 Curse" began [evidence for this hypothesised association?]. Attributing causes helps give us order and predictability to our lives [evidence for this?]. Causal attribution helps us feel better [evidence for this?] by giving predictability to an unpredictable world, but our attributions are not always completely accurate [an example of 'completely accurate,' please].[27]

Humanists, atheists and scientists say that humans make meaning out of just about anything to counter the essential meaningless of the universe. Which is, by their own standards, an untested assumption, a way of explaining to themselves why the poor primitives who believe in such things keep holding onto irrational, unsubstantiated, unscientific, religious beliefs which, to modern minds, are obviously false.

Sceptics slaver at things like the 27 Club. They think it's like shooting fish in a barrel, popping irrational balloons with sober facts. But somehow 7 billion humans just keep on seeing pattern, making meaning, doing things that are

[27] Why Have Famous Musicians Died at 27? *Psychology Today.* www.psychologytoday.com/blog/here-there-and-everywhere/ 201107/why-have-famous-musicians-died-27

"irrational" like getting married, having children, making mistakes, falling in love, or investing in the stock market.

Stages of life

The stages of the human lifespan are an archetype. And they are stages—platforms where we jump off into the next adventure, where we play out the comedy or a tragedy that is our life. Shakespeare called them the seven stages of man, peopled with archetypes: the infant, the schoolboy, the lover, the soldier, the justice, the old man, and death.

> All the world's a stage,
> And all the men and women merely players;
> They have their exits and their entrances,
> And one man in his time plays many parts,
> His acts being seven ages. At first, the infant,
> Mewling and puking in the nurse's arms.
> Then the whining schoolboy, with his satchel
> And shining morning face, creeping like snail
> Unwillingly to school. And then the lover,
> Sighing like furnace, with a woeful ballad
> Made to his mistress' eyebrow. Then a soldier,
> Full of strange oaths and bearded like the pard,
> Jealous in honour, sudden and quick in quarrel,
> Seeking the bubble reputation
> Even in the cannon's mouth.
> And then the justice,
> In fair round belly with good capon lined,
> With eyes severe and beard of formal cut,
> Full of wise saw and modern instances;
> And so he plays his part. The sixth age shifts
> Into the lean and slippered pantaloon

With spectacles on nose and pouch on side;
His youthful hose, well saved, a world too wide
For his shrunk shank, and his big manly voice,
Turning again toward childish treble, pipes
And whistles in his sound. Last scene of all,
That ends this strange eventful history,
Is second childishness and mere oblivion,
Sans teeth, sans eyes, sans taste, sans everything.
—Jacques, *As You Like It*, William Shakespeare

In the first half of the 20th century psychology's focus was mainly on child development. From the 1960s to the 1990s there was a blossoming of interest and research into adult development. Developmental researchers such as Erik Erikson, James Fowler, Roger Gould, Lawrence Kohlberg, Daniel Levinson, Jane Loevinger, Bernice Neugarten, and George Valliant, and family life cycle researchers such as Monica McGoldrick, Betty Carter, Celia Falicov and Florence Kaslow, put forward stage theories of development that roughly coincide with the Moon Cycles. To mention a few:

Erik Erikson, a psychoanalyst, wrote about the crucial turning points in human development as: 15–22 years, identity and role confusion; 18–28, intimacy versus isolation; 25–45, generativity versus stagnation; and 45 and up, ego integrity versus despair (maturity).

Gail Sheehy in her book *Passages* labels the stages as pulling up roots (18–22), the trying twenties (22–28), catch 30 (28–32), rooting (32–39), deadline decade (35–45), and renewal or resignation (mid-forties onwards).

Rudolf Steiner, who founded Anthroposophy, spoke of mental, emotional and spiritual development proceeding in 7-year stages (0–7, 7–14, 14–21, 21–28 and so on).

Nicholas Weiler and Stephen Schoonover describe the life stages of the twenties:[28]Autonomy and Tentative Choices (18–26)—developing personal autonomy and leaving the family; developing our own sense of personhood as separate from parents and childhood peer groups; trying out new relationships; typically a period of tentative or provisional commitments; comfortable that there is plenty of time ahead to change our minds. Young Adult Transition (27–31)—usually a period of significant turmoil and asking if we're really journeying in directions we want to go. Have we made the right decisions? Are we running out of time to change our decisions? Are our decisions becoming permanent before we want them to? Often with considerable angst similar to the better known mid-life.

Psychiatrist Roger Gould, in his book *Transformations,* said:

> From 16 to 22 youngsters are condensed energy looking for a direction and looking for rules to break. The task is to break away from real or perceived parental control. Romance and intimacy outside the family is an attempt to cut loose from parents without losing a sense of safety and belonging. From 22 to 28, optimism, determination and confidence are high. Careers are pursued without much introspection. The young adults wrestle with the false assumption that 'rewards will come automatically if I do what I am supposed to do.' From 28 to 34 is a time of disillusionment and soul searching. Life is viewed as complicated and unfair. Discovering that 'life is a struggle' is like rediscovering the wheel.

---

[28] Nicholas Weiler and Stephen Schoonover. *Your Soul at Work: Five Steps to a More Fulfilling Career and Life.*

What Gould points to is like second-season syndrome. The first season (24–27) the player does well and scores lots of goals, tries or points but during the second season (27–30) he goes into a slump. The mark of the best players is that they are able to live through this.

When all these frameworks are overlapped, we get something like: Leaving the family (16–22). Reaching out (23–28). Questions, questions (29–34). Mid-life explosion (35–43). Settling down (44–50). Mellowing (50 plus).

Common to all the above theories are several years of high energy and exploration in the mid-twenties, then a shift of gears in the late twenties around 28 followed by a period of introspection and reorientation. The Moon Cycles say that at age 27.9 we enter the south the Little Centre Moon of the Big West Moon. That's the place of the birth of the catalyst of death and change.

Neuroscience

In a baby, the brain over-produces brain cells (neurons) and connections between brain cells (synapses) and then starts pruning them back around the age of three. The process is much like the pruning of a tree—by cutting back weak branches, others are enabled to flourish. The second wave of over-production shows a spurt of growth in the frontal cortex just before puberty (around age 11 in girls, 12 in boys) and then a pruning back in adolescence.

Sophisticated imaging studies and other research show that the frontal lobe of the brain—the part involved in judgment, organisation, planning and strategising—gets all its grey matter by age 11 or 12. But the myriad connections from the frontal part aren't completely wired to function like an adult for at least another decade.

The prefrontal cortex, the part of the frontal lobes lying just behind the forehead, is the CEO of the brain. This region is responsible for cognitive analysis and abstract thought, and the moderation of "correct" behaviour in social situations. The prefrontal cortex takes in information from all of the senses and orchestrates thoughts and actions to achieve specific goals.

The brain matures from back to front and the prefrontal cortex is one of the last regions of the brain to reach maturation. The "executive functions" of the human prefrontal cortex include: focusing attention; organising thoughts and problem solving; foreseeing and weighing possible consequences of behaviour; considering the future and making predictions; forming strategies and planning; ability to balance short-term rewards with long term goals; impulse control and delaying gratification; inhibiting inappropriate behaviour and initiating appropriate behaviour; and the modulation of intense emotions. In other words, "good judgment."

The poor judgment exhibited in adolescence and early adulthood goes along with an immature prefrontal cortex. The inability to anticipate future consequences of current actions is a hallmark of youth. Binge drinking in adolescence is associated with a smaller prefrontal cortex. Whether the drinking is the cause of, or the result of, a reduced prefrontal cortex is not known.[29]

"According to recent findings," the Young Adult Development Project at the Massachusetts Institute of Technology says, "the human brain does not reach full maturity until at least the mid-20s.... As a number of researchers have put it, 'the rental car companies have it right.' The brain isn't

---

[29] "Smaller Prefrontal Cortex Is Associated with Early-onset Drinking." www.news-medical.net/news/2005/09/26/13250.aspx

fully mature at 16, when we are allowed to drive, or at 18, when we are allowed to vote, or at 21, when we are allowed to drink, but closer to 25, when we are allowed to rent a car."[30]

Research

There is very little research on the 27 Club. Not surprisingly most of it does not support the existence of the Club. Mark Bellis, of the Centre for Public Health, Liverpool John Moores University, looked at early deaths of rock stars. He found that from 3 to 25 years post-fame, both North American and European pop stars experience two to three times higher mortality rates than demographically matched populations in the USA and UK, respectively. After 25 years of fame, relative mortality in European (but not North American) pop stars begins to return to population levels. Chronic drug- or alcohol-related problems or overdose was identified as associated with over a quarter of deaths.[31] In other words, being a rock star is a high risk job when you are younger. But if you survive you'll be OK-ish.

Dianna Kenny, Professor of Psychology, University of Sydney, carried out an informal study on musician's deaths. She said, "The idea of the 27 Club has been imprinted into the collective imagination.... But other investigations into the 27 Club, have concluded that the age of 27 does not

[30] "Young Adult Development Project." http://hrweb.mit.edu/worklife/youngadult/brain.html#beyond

[31] Bellis, Mark et al. "Elvis to Eminem: Quantifying the Price of Fame Through Early Mortality of European and North American Rock and Pop Stars." *Journal of Epidemiology and Community Health*, 2007, 61 (10) (October 1): 896-901. doi:10.1136/jech.2007.059915.

bestow any greater risk of death in popular musicians than other ages."[32]

In 2011 Martin Wolkewitz and others (University of Freiburg and Queensland University of Technology) studied 1046 solo artists and band members who had a number one album in the UK between 1956–2007. They found that: "There was no peak in risk around age 27, but the risk of death for famous musicians throughout their 20s and 30s was two to three times higher than the general UK population. The 27 Club is unlikely to be a real phenomenon. Fame may increase the risk of death among musicians, but this risk is not limited to age 27."[33]

For the record, I will list some of the common arguments against the existence of the 27 Club: The majority of famous musicians, many of whom who have admitted to past drug use, have lived well past 27 years old. The members of the 27 Club had a history of drug use which is strongly associated with health problems and impaired judgement and a greater chance of death. Famous musicians tend to do things that the general population does not. For example, flying in small aircraft, and more frequently. From this we would expect an increased mortality as a result of small plane crashes. There are a number of rock stars musicians who died at 21, but there is no "21 Club Curse." The deaths (especially unexpected ones) of famous people tend to be more memorable and more newsworthy. Musicians often become famous in their early twenties and their risk-taking peaks four to five years later. The 27 Club exists by chance

---

[32] www.independent.co.uk/arts-entertainment/music/features/ why-the-27-club-is-a-myth-jimi-hendrix-and-amy-winehouse-may-be-members-but-that-doesnt-make-it-real-10152675

[33] Is 27 Really a Dangerous Age for Famous Musicians? Retrospective Cohort Study, Br Medical J. http://www.bmj.com/content/343/bmj.d7799.

and is an example of confirmation bias, where people focus on results that support their belief and ignore those that refute it.

But I will give the last word on this to Eric Segalstad, author of *The 27s: The Greatest Myth of Rock and Roll.* In an interview in 2009 he said:

> I don't really believe in… well, I'm very factual. Both my parents are scientists…. As I've gotten older, I've realized that there are a lot of things I can't explain, that people, like mankind, might not be able to understand or explain…. So I looked at the [Liverpool] research methodology and went through and found that they had fourteen 27s on their list. I guessed that would be the highest number by far out of any other age, more so than 28s, 33s or 56s. So I called up the doctor in charge of the research [to verify], and he told me that, yes, that was the case. He couldn't explain it. But that was the case. It's a weird outlier."[34]

---

[34] http://www.7dvt.com/2009dying-get.

7

The 27 Club (Slight Return)

The loveliest and the last
The bloom, whose petals nipped before they blew
Died on the promise of the fruit.
                    —*Adonais*, elegy for John Keats
                            by Percy Bysshe Shelley

Let me die a youngman's death
not a clean and inbetween
the sheets holywater death
not a famous-last-words
peaceful out of breath death...
Let me die a youngman's death
not a free from sin tiptoe in
candle wax and waning death
not a curtains drawn by angels borne
'what a nice way to go' death
                            —Roger McGough

Well I stand up next to a mountain
and chop it down with the edge of my hand.
            —Jimi Hendrix, *Voodoo Child (Slight Return)*

I have attempted to outline the psychological forces that merge and emerge in our late twenties. The Moon Cycles give us a hint about the timing of these challenges. For most of us these matters go either unnoticed or unnamed in the churn of life and, like the physiology of the body, work outside our conscious awareness. But, like physical illness, it's only when things go wrong that we are forced to look at what might be happening underneath the surface of our psyche.

The Other Clubs

The drug use associated with being a rock star; its disinhibiting effect on a not-yet-quite-matured prefrontal cortex; always living close to the edge; the inflation and grandiosity of success and money; high-flying puer traits; living out the archetype of the young and dying god; chance, luck and fate; pre-existing or emerging depression or other psychological difficulties; the kairos of the Moon Cycles, all make for a perfect storm around 27.

But the storms of the twenties are not local to age 27. There is the 24 Club, the 25 Club, the 26 Club, and so on. Each has its own face and voice.

The 24 Club

The Illumination of the Choices and Decisions of of Childhood and the Little Chaotic Journey into the Little East Moon of Illumination. This Little Moon from 24–27 precedes the final moon of the Big South.

Andrew Wood (24 years, 2 months, 11 days, January 8, 1966–March 19, 1990). Lead singer for grunge bands Malfunkshun and Mother Love Bone. Heroin overdose.

Berry Oakley (24 years 7 months 7 days, April 4, 1948–November 11, 1972). Bassist and founding member of The Allman Brothers Band. When Duane Allman died in a motorcycle accident, Oakley was devastated and started drinking heavily. He died in a motorcycle accident in Macon, Georgia, just three blocks from where Allman had died the year before.

Cliff Burton (24 years 7 months 17 days, February 10, 1962–September 27, 1986). Bass guitarist for Metallica. When the band's tour bus overturned in rural southern Sweden.

Duane Allman (24 years 11 months 9 days, November 20, 1946–October 29, 1971). Co-founder of the Allman Brothers Band. Motorcycle accident.

James Dean (24 years 7 months 22 days, February 8, 1931–September 30, 1955). Film actor in only three films (East of Eden, Giant, and Rebel Without a Cause). Car crash.

Louise Dean (24 years 2 months 14 days, April 4, 1971–June 18, 1995). Singer for UK dance band Shiva. Hit and run accident.

Matthew Jay (24 years 11 months 15 days, October 10, 1978–September 25, 2003). English singer-songwriter likened to artists such as Nick Drake, Badly Drawn Boy and Jeff Buckley. Unexplained fall from the 7th storey of an apartment building.

Nicholas "Razzle" Dingley (24 years 0 months 7 days, December 2, 1960–December 9, 1984). Drummer for Finnish band Hanoi Rocks. Car accident. Had a cross tattoo with "Too fast to live, too young to die."

Peter Laughner (24 years 11 months 0 days, August 22, 1952–June 22, 1977). American guitarist, songwriter and singer, Pere Ubu. Acute pancreatitis as a result of drug and alcohol abuse.

Stefanie Sargent (24 years 0 months 19 days, June 8, 1968–June 27, 1992). Guitarist for Seattle punk band 7 Year Bitch. Asphyxiated on her own vomit.

Steve "Pre" Prefontaine (24 years 4 months 5 days, January 25, 1951–May 30, 1975). American middle and long-distance runner. Prefontaine once held USA records from 2,000 metres to 10,000 metres. Car accident. He has been posthumously nicknamed "the James Dean of track" because both men had a reputation as rebels and loners, and both of them died in auto accidents (in convertibles) at the age of 24.

The 25 Club

The Death and Change of the Illumination of Childhood

> Well Billy rapped all night about his suicide
> How he kicked it in the head when he was twenty-five
> Speed jive don't want to stay alive
> When you're twenty-five
> —Mott the Hoople, "All the Young Dudes"
> by David Bowie

> Angels fight, angels cry, angels dance and angels die
> I lose my mind with faraway eyes
> It just feels like I'm paralyzed
> Turning 25 thinking of suicide
> — Hardcore Superstar, "Rock 'n' Roll Star"

Frankie Lymon (25 years 4 months 28 days, September 30, 1942–February 27, 1968). Lead singer, The Teenagers. Their first single in 1956, "Why Do Fools Fall in Love," was also their biggest hit. Heroin overdose.

James Honeyman-Scott (25 years 7 months 12 days, November 4, 1956–June 16, 1982). English rock guitarist, songwriter and founding member of The Pretenders. Heart failure from cocaine overdose.

John Keats (25 years 3 months 23 days, October 31, 1795–February 23, 1821). English Romantic poet and contemporary of Lord Byron and Percy Bysshe Shelley. Author of Ode to a Grecian Urn, To Autumn, The Eve of St Agnes, and Endymion. Of tuberculosis. Seven weeks after Keats' funeral and 18 months before his own death Shelley wrote "Adonais."

Johnny Ace (25 years 6 months 16 days, June 9, 1929–December 25, 1954). American rhythm and blues singer. Self-inflicted gunshot wound on Christmas Day.

Justin Charles Pierce (25 years 3 months 19 days, March 21, 1975–July 10, 2000). English-born American actor and professional skateboarder. Suicide by hanging.

Ken "Dimwit" Montgomery (c. 25 years, 1958–September 27, 1994). Drummer for Vancouver hardcore punk band D.O.A., often referred to as the founders of hardcore punk. Heroin overdose.

Matthew Fletcher (25 years 7 months 9 days, November 5, 1970–June 14, 1996). Drummer for UK pop bands Talulah Gosh and Heavenly. Suicide.

Oystein "Euronymous" Aarseth (25 years 4 months 19 days, March 22, 1968–August 10, 1993). Norwegian guitarist and co-founder of black metal band Mayhem. Murdered by fellow musician Varg Vikernes.

Paul Kossoff (25 years 6 months 5 days, September 14, 1950–March 19, 1976). English guitarist, Free. Son of David Kossoff, the British actor of Russian-Jewish descent. Died on a flight from Los Angeles to New York from drug-related heart problems.

Randy Rhoads (25 years 3 months 13 days, December 6, 1956–March 19, 1982). American heavy metal guitarist who played with Ozzy Osbourne and Quiet Riot. Light airplane crash as a result of trying to "buzz" the tour bus.

Richard "Tommy" Bolin (25 years 4 months 3 days, August 1, 1951–December 4, 1976). American-born guitarist who played with Zephyr, The James Gang, and Deep Purple. Heroin overdose.

Tupac Shakur (25 years 2 months 28 days, June 16, 1971–September 13, 1996). American rapper. Murdered.

Wilfred Owen MC (25 years 7 months 17 days, March 18, 1893–November 4, 1918,). One of the leading poets of the First World War. Killed in action crossing the Sambre–Oise Canal, exactly one week (almost to the hour) before the signing of the Armistice.

The 26 Club

The Wisdom and Knowledge of the Illumination of Childhood

Casey Calvert (26 years 1 month 2 days, October 22, 1981–November 24, 2007). Lead guitarist of Hawthorne Heights. Fatal drug interaction of Citalopram, Clonazepam and Vicodin.

Gram Parsons (26 years 10 months 14 days, November 5, 1946–September 19, 1973). American singer, songwriter, guitarist and pianist of The Byrds and The Flying Burrito Brothers. Overdose of morphine and alcohol in Joshua Tree National Park.

Hillel Slovak (26 years 2 months 12 days, April 13, 1962–June 25, 1988). Israeli-American guitarist and founding member of the Red Hot Chili Peppers. Heroin overdose.

Jimmy McCulloch (26 years 3 months 23 days, June 4, 1953–September 24, 1979). Scottish lead guitar in Paul McCartney's Wings from 1974 to 1977. Heart failure from heroin overdose.

Malcolm Owen (c. 26 years, Unknown–July 14, 1980). Lead singer for UK punk band The Ruts. Heroin overdose.

Nick Drake (26 years 5 months 6 days, June 19, 1948–November 25, 1974). English singer-songwriter and musician. In the 1980s he came to represent the "doomed romantic." Overdose of Amitryptiline.

Otis Redding (26 years 3 months 1 day, September 9, 1941–December 10, 1967). American soul singer-songwriter and record producer. Small plane crash near Madison, Wisconsin on his way to a gig.

Petri Ilari Walli (26 years, 4 months, 3 days, February 25, 1969–June 28, 1995). Founder of Finnish psychedelic rock band Kingston Wall. Suicide by jumping off the balcony of the Toololo Church, Helsinki.

The 27 Club

The Double Illumination of Childhood and the Big Chaotic Journey into the Big West Moon of Death and Change. At age 27.0 we leave the Big Moon of Trust and Innocence and travel on a Chaotic Journey for nine months into the next Big Moon of Death and Change. Before we leave we sit in the East of the East Little Moon of the Big Moon and see (consciously or unconsciusly) in the light of the sun, the last 3 years or the last 27 years of our lives.

Jones, Hendrix, Joplin, Cobain
Sex, money, liquor, cocaine

Rock, Roll, Peace, Love
Now welcome to the 27 club

—XV (aka Donavan Johnson)

Jimi Hendrix (27 years 9 months 22 days, November 27, 1942–September 18, 1970). American guitarist. Died in a London hotel room after asphyxiating on his own vomit, likely a result of combining sleeping pills with wine. His German girlfriend, Monika Danneman, found his body. She inherited Hendrix's estate. In 1996, in the face of a libel action, Dannemann committed suicide by carbon monoxide poisoning.

The quality of the puer, both light and dark (which always go together), is beautifully captured by Pete Townshend's homage to Hendrix, voted No. 1 of the top 100 guitarists of all time by *Rolling Stone*:

He had a kind of alchemist's ability; when he was on the stage, he changed. He physically changed. He became incredibly graceful and beautiful. He was dusty—he had cobwebs and dust all over him. He was shy and kind and sweet, and he was fucked up and insecure.… With Jimi, I didn't have any envy. I never had any sense that I could ever come close.... I felt The Who were in some ways quite a silly little group, that they were indeed my art-school installation.… You know, you smash a guitar, you walk off and go, "Fuck it all. It's all a load of tripe anyway." That really was the beginning of punk consciousness. And then Jimi arrived with proper music.[30]

On August 29, 1970, the day before the Isle of Wight music festival (his last ever gig in the UK), Hendrix told UK music paper Melody Maker:

> It's all turned full circle. I'm back right now to where I started. I've given this era of music everything. I still sound the same, my music's still the same, and I can't think of anything new to add to it.... I want a big band. I don't mean three harps and fourteen violins, I mean a big band full of competent musicians that I can conduct and write for. And with the music we will paint pictures of earth and space, so that the listener can be taken somewhere.

"I'm not sure I'll live to be 28 years-old," Hendrix told journalist Ann Bjorndal just before a disastrous concert in Aarhus, Denmark. "I feel I have nothing more to give musically. I will not be around on this planet any more, unless I have a wife and children—otherwise I've got nothing to live for." At Aarhus, he cut short his set after only three numbers.

On September 6, 1970 Hendrix played what was to be his last gig at The Love + Peace Festival on the island of Fehmarn, off the coast of northern Germany in the Baltic Sea. After heavy rain and gale-force winds the day before, the last two songs Hendrix ever played live were Purple Haze and a stormy version of Voodoo Child (Slight Return). The final lines of the song, and the final words that Hendrix would ever sing in public, were: "If I don't see you no more in this world / I'll meet you in the next one and don't be late, don't be late."[31]

Jim Morrison (27 years 6 months 25 days, December 8, 1943–July 3, 1971). Lyricist and singer of The Doors. He was the rock poet-philosopher who drank and drugged heavily.

Five to one, baby, one in five, no one here gets out alive. —"Five to One," Waiting for the Sun

I am the Lizard King, I can do anything.
    —"Not to Touch the Earth," *Waiting for the Sun*

The difference between Jim Morrison and Elvis Presley is that Elvis had humility. I don't think Jim had it.
    —Patti Smith

Morrison's angry relationship with his father and his rejection of his authority were well-known. At the height of Morrison's fame, and at the height of the Vietnam War, his father was the commander of US aircraft carriers in the Gulf of Tonkin.

Tired of his celebrity status, Morrison and his long-time girlfriend Pamela Courson moved to Paris in March 1971 and lived in a house formerly owned by poet Arthur Rimbaud. Four months later Courson found him dead in the bathroom of their apartment. A heroin overdose was suspected. Three years later on April 25, 1974 Courson was found dead in her L.A. apartment of a heroin overdose. She was 27.

Janis Joplin (27 years 8 months 15 days, January 19, 1943–October 4, 1970). Singer (Down On Me, Summertime, Piece of My Heart, Ball 'n' Chain, Try (Just A Little Bit Harder), Mercedes-Benz, Me and Bobby McGee) with

Big Brother and the Holding Company, The Kozmic Blues Band, The Full Tilt Boogie Band, and Pearl.

While in high school in Port Arthur, Texas, Joplin said, "I was a misfit. I read, I painted, I didn't hate niggers." While at the University of Texas she was nominated "Ugliest Man on Campus." She was bisexual and had a life-long sense of inferiority which she compensated for by having relationships with some of the most desirable men of the time—including Joe Namath, Kris Kristofferson, Jim Morrison, and Dick Cavett.

Joplin moved to San Francisco in 1966 and joined Big Brother and the Holding Company. They stole the show at the Monterey International Pop Festival in June 1967. The line-up was a Who's Who of the 1960s—The Mamas and Papas, The Association, The Who, The Byrds, The Paul Butterfield Blues Band, Scott McKenzie, Canned Heat, Buffalo Springfield, Johnny Rivers, Electric Flag, Eric Burdon and the Animals, Simon and Garfunkel, Jefferson Airplane, Country Joe and the Fish, The Grateful Dead, Steve Miller Band, Quicksilver Messenger Service, Moby Grape, Lou Rawls, Otis Redding, Booker T and the MGs, Hugh Masakela, Laura Nyro, and Ravi Shankar.

In mid-1970 she became engaged to Seth Morgan, an heir to the Ivory Soap fortune. Just before her death she was involved in recording her album Pearl—the nickname she took for the hard-living, blues-mama persona she had adopted. On October 4, 1970 she was found dead in a Los Angeles motel room of a heroin overdose with alcohol. It was 16 days after Jimi Hendrix died.

Kurt Cobain (27 years 1 month 16 days, February 20, 1967–
    April 5, 1994). Founding member, lead singer, guitarist

and songwriter for Nirvana. Suicide by heroin overdose and gunshot to the head.

I'm going to be a superstar musician, kill myself, and go out in a flame of glory... I want to be rich and famous and kill myself like Jimi Hendrix.

—Kurt Cobain

I'm not worried about what's going to happen when I'm thirty, because I am never going to make it to thirty. You know what life is like after thirty, I don't want that. —Kurt Cobain

There was no control to the burn.

—Neil Young on Kurt Cobain

Cobain's parents divorced when he was seven. "I had a really good childhood," he recalled, "and then all of a sudden my whole world changed. I remember feeling ashamed. I became anti-social. People just left me alone.... I always felt that they would vote me Most Likely to Kill Everyone at a High School Dance."

Grunge in the USA was born from British punk rock. Adopting the personae of traumatised children Nirvana became role models for the twentysomething "slackers" of Generation X and in turn they bore offspring such as Pearl Jam and Stone Temple Pilots. Cobain was deeply conflicted about Nirvana's success. The lyrics of *In Utero*, their third and last album said, "Teenage angst has paid off well. Now I'm bored and old."[33] He was found at his Seattle home by an electrician who had arrived to install a security system.

Amy Winehouse (27 years 10 months 9 days, September 14, 1983–July 23, 2011). Singer (R&B, jazz and soul music) and songwriter known for her smoky contralto.

Newsweek said she was "a perfect storm of sex kitten, raw talent and poor impulse control." In 2006 she had a hit single "Rehab," about her refusal to attend an alcohol rehabilitation program. Her album *Back to Black* led to five Grammy Awards in 2008. But her performances got more shambolic. At Glastonbury she staggered about the stage and was heckled by the crowd.

After drinking for several days, she was found in her bed by her bodyguard. The coroner's report said she had 416 mg per 100 ml blood alcohol level. 350 mg was considered fatal.

On what would have been her 28th birthday her father, Mitch Winehouse, said that neither Amy's family, friends nor doctors saw her death coming. "Nobody could have foreseen what would [sic] have happened."[37]

If Hendrix was the blazing star; Morrison, the moody poet; Joplin, the good-time girl, then Cobain and Winehouse were the ones most openly intent on self-destruction. Of all The 27 Club members Winehouse most clearly approximated what clinicians call borderline personality disorder. Whether she was diagnostically borderline is not our concern here, but she had a borderline life and borderline relationships.

The fascination with, fury with (think Ted Hughes post-Sylvia Plath), and sentimentality about young death is part of the archetype—the nostalgic yearning for "What if…" and "If only…"; the zippered rage at the waste; the knifing loss of bright, bright beauty; the wish for death not to cut life short, at any age; and the razor reminder that all dreams are never fulfilled, completely. In the obits we hear the defensive certainty that it could have been different, the tut-tutting about the shame of it all, and the desperate denial of death.

Other 27s

Alan "Blind Owl" Wilson (27 years 1 month 20 days, July 14, 1943–September 3, 1970). Singer, guitarist, and harmonica player for Canned Heat. Barbiturate overdose.

Alexander Bashlachev (27 years 8 months 23 days, May 27, 1960–February 17, 1988). Russian poet, musician, guitarist, and singer-songwriter. Jumped from the ninth floor window of his apartment on Kuznetsova Avenue in Leningrad.

Alexandra (27 years 2 months 13 days, May 19, 1942–July 31, 1969). German pop singer. Car accident.

Andres Escobar (27 years 3 months 19 days, March 13, 1967–July 2, 1994). Colombian soccer player. Shot outside a bar in a suburb of Medellin, Colombia. Possibly in retaliation for scoring an own goal in a World Cup match which resulted in Colombia's elimination from the tournament and heavy gambling losses for the Colombian drug underworld.

Andrew Cunanan (27 years 10 months 23 days, August 31, 1969–July 23, 1997). Cunanan's killing spree over three months placed him on the FBI "most wanted" list. His last victim was Gianni Versace. Suicide by gunshot eight days later.

Arlester "Dyke" Christian (27 years 9 months 4 days, June 13, 1943–March 13, 1971). Frontman, vocalist and bassist of the first funk band Dyke & the Blazers. Shot several times while sitting in his car in downtown Phoenix.

Brian Jones (27 years 4 months 5 days, February 28, 1942–July 3, 1969). Founder and guitarist for the Rolling Stones. Drowned in the swimming pool of his home at Cotchford Farm, Hartfield, Sussex (once owned by Winnie-the-Pooh author, A. A. Milne). The coroner recorded "Death by misadventure" and noted his liver and heart were enlarged by drug and alcohol abuse. Mick Jagger and Keith Richards had taken over as the Stones' leaders and Jones was told that Mick Taylor would replace him. He died a month later.

Bobby Bloom (27 years 9 months 6 days, May 22, 1946–February 28, 1974). American singer-songwriter best known for a 1970 one-hit wonder Montego Bay. Suffered from depression towards the end of his life. Shot himself while cleaning his gun.

Bobby Sands (27 years 1 month 26 days, March 9, 1954–May 5, 1981). Irish Republican Army member. After conviction for firearms possession, Sands became the leader of a hunger strike by Irish republican prisoners to regain status as political rather than criminal prisoners. Died of self-imposed starvation in Maze Prison after a 66-day hunger strike.

Bryan Ottoson (27 years 1 month 1 day, March 18, 1978–April 19, 2005). Guitarist for American Head Charge. Prescription drug overdose.

Chris Bell (27 years 11 months 15 days, January 12, 1951–December 27, 1978). American singer, songwriter and guitarist. Along with Alex Chilton (The Box Tops) he led the power pop band Big Star. Leaving the band in 1972, he struggled with depression and heroin. Killed when his Triumph TR-6 struck a wooden power pole.

Damien Morris (27 years 7 months, c. April 1980–December 19, 2007). Singer, Australian death metal band, The Red Shore. Tour bus crash.

Dave Alexander (27 years 8 months 8 days, June 3, 1947–February 10, 1975). Original bassist for The Stooges. Died of pulmonary edema after being hospitalised for pancreatitis from years of drinking.

Dennes Boon (27 years 8 months 21 days, April 1, 1958–December 22, 1985). American singer and guitarist of punk band The Minutemen. Thrown out the back door of a van when it ran off the road in the Arizona desert.

Dickie Pride (27 years 5 months 5 days, October 21, 1941–March 26, 1969). British rock 'n' roll singer, contemporary of Marty Wilde and Billy Fury. Overdose of sleeping pills.

Fat Pat (27 years 1 month 30 days, December 4, 1970–February 3, 1998). Rapper and member of Screwed Up Click. Murdered.

Gary Thain (27 years 6 months 23 days, May 15, 1948–December 8, 1975). New Zealand-born bassist for the Keef Hartley Band and Uriah Heep. On September 15, 1974 he suffered electric shock onstage at the Moody Coliseum in Dallas, Texas and was seriously injured. Heroin overdose.

Helmut Kollen (27 years 2 months 1 day, March 2, 1950–May 3, 1977). Bassist and singer for German progressive rock band Triumvirat. A mechanic and race car driver, Kollen died from carbon monoxide poisoning listening to studio mixes in his car running with the garage door shut.

Jean-Michel Basquiat (27 years 7 months 21 days, December 22, 1960–August 12, 1988). American artist. Friend of Andy Warhol. David Bowie played Warhol in the 1996 film *Basquiat*. Heroin overdose.

Jeremy Michael Ward (27 years 0 months 20 days, May 5, 1976–May 25, 2003). The Mars Volta and De Facto sound operator. Heroin overdose.

Jesse Belvin (27 years 1 month 22 days, December 15, 1932–February 6, 1960). R&B singer, pianist and songwriter ("Earth Angel," "Goodnight My Love") popular in the 1950s. Car crash in Hope, Arkansas.

John Garrighan (27 years 9 months 29 days, April 1, 1983–January 30, 2011). Guitarist and vocalist for punk band The Berlin Project. Heroin overdose.

Jonathan Gregory Brandis (27 years 6 months 30 days, April 13, 1976–November 12, 2003). American actor in The Never Ending Story II and SeaQuest DSV. Suicide by hanging.

Kristen Pfaff (27 years 0 months 21 days, May 26, 1967–June 16, 1994). Bassist for Hole. Heroin overdose.

Les Harvey (27 years 7 months 20 days, September 13, 1944–May 3, 1972). Scottish co-founding guitarist for Stone The Crows and a member of The Alex Harvey Soul Band. Electrocuted by an ungrounded microphone after touching it with his wet hands.

Malcolm Hale (27 years 5 months 13 days, May 17, 1941–October 30, 1968). Lead guitarist and trombonist for Spanky & Our Gang ("Sunday Will Never Be The Same" and "Lazy Day.") Carbon monoxide poisoning from a faulty space heater.

Mia Zapata (27 years 10 months 12 days, August 25, 1965–July 7, 1993). Lead singer, Seattle punk band The Gits. Raped, beaten and strangled.

Pat Tillman (27 years 5 months 16 days, November 6, 1976–April 22, 2004). American football player and US

Army Ranger. In May 2002 Tillman turned down a of $3.6 million contract offer from the Arizona Cardinals and enlisted in the US Army. Killed by "friendly fire" in Afghanistan.

Pete de Freitas (27 years 10 months 12 days, August 2, 1961–June 14, 1989). Drummer of Echo and the Bunnymen. Motorcycle accident.

Pete Ham (27 years 11 months 28 days, April 27, 1947–April 24, 1975). Keyboardist and guitarist, Welsh rock band Badfinger. Suicide by hanging.

Randy "Stretch" Walker (27 years 3 months 9 days, August 21, 1968–November 30, 1995). American hip hop rapper, founder of Live Squad in the late 1980s. Murdered.

Raymond "Freaky Tah" Rogers (27 years 10 months 14 days, May 14, 1971–March 28, 1999). Lost Boyz hip hop group. Murdered.

Richey Edwards (27 years 1 month 10 days, December 22, 1967–c. February 1, 1995). Welsh lyricist and guitarist for the Manic Street Preachers. Disappeared from his London hotel, his abandoned car was found two weeks later near the Severn Bridge, a well-known suicide spot. He was presumed dead in 2008 by his family.

Robert Johnson (27 years 3 months 8 days, May 8, 1911–August 16, 1938). Legendary Mississippi bluesman and songwriter (Travelling Riverside Blues, Last Fair Deal Gone Down, If I Had Possession Over Judgment Day, Love in Vain, Hellhound on My Trail, Sweet Home Chicago, Cross Road Blues). Drank whiskey laced with strychnine at a country crossroads near Greenwood, Mississippi. When Keith Richards first heard Johnson, he was convinced it wasn't a solo guitarist. "Who's the other guy?" he asked. Eric Clapton said, "Up until I was 25, if you didn't know who Robert Johnson was, I wouldn't talk to you."

Roger Durham (27 years 5 months 13 days, February 14, 1946–July 27, 1973). Percussionist for American R&B group Bloodstone. From injuries falling off a horse.

Ron "Pigpen" McKernan (27 years 6 months 0 days, September 8, 1945–March 8, 1973). Keyboardist and founding member of the Grateful Dead. Stomach haemorrhage from years of heavy drinking.

Rudy Lewis (27 years 8 months 27 days, August 23, 1936–May 20, 1964). Lead singer for The Drifters. Choked to death in his sleep. Suspected drug overdose.

Rupert Brooke (27 years 8 months 20 days, August 3, 1887–April 23, 1915). English poet, known for his idealistic sonnets written during WWI. Died of sepsis from an infected mosquito bite on a British Navy ship off Lemnos in the Aegean Sea en route to Gallipoli.

Sean McCabe (27 years 9 months 15 days, November 13, 1972–August 28, 2000). Lead singer for the hardcore punk band Ink and Dagger. Choked to death on his own vomit.

The 28 Club

Death and Change of the Catalyst of Death and Change. After our Chaotic Journey we reach the South of the Little Centre Moon of the Big West Moon. From 27.9 to age 30 we walk around the moon of the Catalyst of Death and Change. How we do this determines the trajectory of the next 27 years.

Brad Nowell (28 years 3 months 3 days, February 22, 1968–May 25, 1996). Lead singer and guitarist of Sublime. Heroin overdose.

Brandon Lee (28 years, 1 month, 30 days, February 1, 1965–March 31, 1993). American actor and martial artist. He was the son of martial arts film star Bruce Lee. Accidentally shot and killed in North Carolina while filming The Crow.

David Kennedy (28 years 10 months 10 days, June 15, 1955–April 25, 1984). Fourth of eleven children of Robert and Ethel Kennedy. Overdose of cocaine, Demerol and Mellaril.

Heath Ledger (28 years, 9 months, 18 days, April 4, 1979–January 22, 2008). Australian actor (Ten Things I Hate About You, The Patriot, and Brokeback Mountain). Acute intoxication from the combined effects of oxycodone, hydrocodone, diazepam, temazepam, alprazolam and doxylamine. He had been suffering from chronic insomnia.

Jason Thirsk (28 years 7 months 4 days, December 25, 1967–July 29, 1996). Bass player for California punk band Pennywise. Self-inflicted gunshot.

Jiles Perry "J.P." Richardson (28 years 3 months 10 days, October 24, 1930–February 3, 1959). DJ, singer and songwriter (Chantilly Lace) aka The Big Bopper. Killed in airplane crash in Iowa along with Buddy Holly and Ritchie Valens. The date has become known as The Day that Music Died (from Don McLean's song, American Pie).

John Glascock (28 years 6 months 15 days, May 2, 1951–November 17, 1979). Bass guitarist and backing vocalist for Jethro Tull. Heart valve defect, resulting from an abscessed tooth.

Richard Shannon Hoon (28 years, 0 months 25 days, September 26, 1967–October 21, 1995). Frontman and lead singer, Blind Melon. Cocaine overdose.

Steven Gaines (28 years 1 month 6 days, September 14, 1949–October 20, 1977). Guitarist and songwriter, Lynyrd Skynyrd. Small airplane crash.

Tim Buckley (28 years 4 months 15 days, February 14, 1947–June 29, 1975). Started as a folk musician but over time incorporated jazz, funk, soul, From heroin, morphine and alcohol overdose. His son Jeff Buckley (30 years 6 months 12 days, November 17, 1966–May 29, 1997) was also a singer who died from accidental drowning when swimming in the Wolf River.

Tracy Pew (28 years 10 months 19 days, December 19, 1957–November 7, 1986). Australian bass player for The Birthday Party. History of epilepsy and heavy drug use. Died of head injuries after epileptic fit.

The 29 Club

The Wisdom and Knowledge of the Catalyst of Death and Change

Brian Cole (29 years 10 months 25 days, September 8, 1942–August 2, 1972). Bass guitar player, founding member of The Association. Heroin overdose.

Clarence White (29 years 1 month 8 days, June 7, 1944–July 15, 1973). Guitar player for The Byrds. Killed by drunk driver.

Danny Whitten (29 years 6 months 10 days, May 8, 1943–November 18, 1972). Songwriter, guitarist for Neil Young's Crazy Horse. Drug overdose.

Hank Williams (29 years 3 months 15 days, September 17, 1923–January 1, 1953). American country music singer-songwriter (Your Cheatin' Heart, Hey, Good Lookin', and I'm So Lonesome I Could Cry). Overdose of morphine and alcohol.

Helno (29 years 0 months 28 days, December 25, 1963–January 22, 1993). Singer French world music/alt rock group, Les Negresses Vertes. Drug overdose.

Ingo Schwichtenberg (29 years 9 months 18 days, May 18, 1965–March 8, 1995). Drummer for German heavy metal band Helloween. Suffered from schizophrenia and drug addiction. Suicide by jumping in front of a subway train.

Ken Jensen (29 years, 1966–Jan. 29, 1995). Vancouver hardcore punk band, D.O.A. House fire.

Marc Bolan (29 years 11 months 18 days, September 30, 1947–September 16, 1977). Lead singer and guitarist for T. Rex. Car crash. Bolan never learned to drive, fearing a premature death.

Mike Hawthorn (29 years 9 months, 13 days, April 10, 1929–January 22, 1959). British racing driver. Winner 1958 Formula One. After winning, Hawthorn immediately announced his retirement, having been badly affected by the death of his close friend and Ferrari team mate Peter Collins. Only months into his retirement Hawthorn died in a high speed road accident on the M1.

Percy Bysshe Shelley (29 years 11 months 4 days, August 4, 1792–July 8, 1822). Major English Romantic poet and famous for his association with John Keats and Lord Byron. Drowned in a sudden storm while sailing back from Livorno to Lerici, Italy, in his schooner, Don Juan.

Ronnie Van Zant (29 years 9 months 5 days, January 15, 1948–October 20, 1977). Founding member of Lynyrd

Skynyrd. Small plane crash. Bandmate Artimus Pyle recalls: "Ronnie told me he would never live to see thirty and that he would go out on the road. Van Zant's father said, "He said to me many times, 'Daddy, I'll never be 30 years old. That's my limit.'"

Tommy Simpson (29 years 7 months 14 days, November 30, 1937–July 13, 1967). The most successful post-war British cyclist. Died on the slopes of Mont Ventoux during the 13th stage of the 1967 Tour de France. The post mortem found amphetamine and alcohol which proved fatal when combined with the high temperatures of the day and the climb of the Ventoux.

The 30 Club

The Illumination of the Catalyst of Death and Change and the Little Chaotic Journey into the Little Southeast Moon of Self-image.

Andy Gibb (30 years 0 months 5 days, March 5, 1958–March 10, 1988). Youngest brother of Barry, Robin, and Maurice Gibb, The Bee Gees. Died of myocarditis caused by a recent viral infection. "He was like a little puppy—so ashamed when he did something wrong. He was all heart, but he didn't have enough muscle to carry through. He wanted everyone to love him." He sought treatment for drug addiction at the Betty Ford Clinic in the mid-1980s.

Chris Acland (30 years 1 month 10 days, September 7, 1966–October 17, 1996). Drummer for Lush. Suicide by hanging.

Criss Oliva (30 years 6 months 14 days, April 3, 1963–October 17, 1993,). Lead guitarist of Savatage. Head-on collision with drunk driver.

Jim Croce (30 years 8 months 10 days, January 10, 1943–September 20, 1973). American singer/songwriter (Bad, Bad Leroy Brown, Time in a Bottle, and I'll Have to Say I Love You in a Song). Light airplane crash.

Johnny Kidd (30 years 9 months 14 days, December 23, 1935–October 7, 1966). English singer and songwriter (Shakin' All Over). Front man for Johnny Kidd and the Pirates. Car crash.

Pete Farndon (30 years 10 months 2 days, June 12, 1952–April 14, 1983). English bassist and founding member of the rock band The Pretenders. Heroin overdose.

Steve Clark (30 years 8 months 16 days, April 23, 1960–January 8, 1991). Lead guitarist for British hard rock band Def Leppard. Multiple drug overdose.

Sylvia Plath (30 years 3 months 15 days, October 27, 1932–February 11, 1963). American poet, novelist and short story writer. She married fellow poet Ted Hughes in 1956 and they lived together first in the United States and then England. After a long struggle with severe depression and a marital separation, Plath committed suicide in 1963 by gas poisoning from her kitchen stove.

Tommy Caldwell (30 years 5 months 19 days, November 9, 1949–April 28, 1980). Bassist, Marshall Tucker Band. Car crash.

This is the End

> This is the end
> Beautiful friend…
> The end of laughter and soft lies
> The end of nights we tried to die
>
> —The Doors, *The End*

For those who are young, famous and vulnerable, the perfect storm may come at night. Walking on the obsidian edge between life and death, loving it, and feeling immortal, death may flick its tail, just because, and they fall.

The mix is different for each individual. Which combination of historical factors and current events produced a particular outcome for a particular person can never be determined. We know from chaos theory that a small change in initial conditions produces large changes in the long-term outcome. Even a small difference in any of the contributing factors listed above may, over the years, have made the difference between Amy Winehouse waking up in the morning after drinking 2 bottles of vodka rather than going into respiratory arrest during the night after drinking 2½ or so bottles.

In contrast, Roger Taylor, drummer for Queen, said in 2011, "It's a dangerous path, no question about it, and a lot of people fall by the wayside. But I always had an in-built sense of survival. I remember every so often thinking: 'Now that's enough.' As for feeling self-important, well, if you have any sense, you know that all the attention you are getting is not so much down to you, it's down to the position you hold. Basically, you are surrounded by people whose living relies on you being well enough to perform."[35]

Each of us lives several lives. First, there is the life that biographers, acquaintances and the public see. This is the record of outer events, dates and times. What we did and where we went. Second, there is the life that close friends, family members and intimate partners see. This may find its way into a biography but intimate details are often redacted for public consumption. Third is the life an individual experiences within him or herself—private thoughts, dreams, fantasies, feelings—that are rarely shared with anyone. Fourth, and this is the kicker, is the unconscious life that even we are unaware of.

Much of what goes into biographies of 27 Club members is taken from the first and maybe the second lives of the subject. Rarely do we hear of life three and never of life four. But it is the archetypal and unconscious forces that show themselves through dreams or crises which have the most power to determine our fate at age 27.

To take a deeper look at the psyches of the 27 Club is beyond the scope of this book, even if it were possible given the perils and errors of psychological biography. To understand, deeply, the threads and tapestry of a lifetime often takes years of exploration in psychotherapy. A book never does justice to a life.

Even from a distance, without knowing the details and the dynamics, we can see that the best-known members of the 27 Club (Jimi Hendrix, Janis Joplin, Jim Morrison, Brian Jones, Amy Winehouse and Kurt Cobain) all wore the robes of the talented, troubled, wounded, inflated, edge-walking, high flyer. They were torn from life by their

---

[35] www.telegraph.co.uk/culture/music/rockandpopmusic/8785343/Being-in-Queen-was-a-privilege.html

own magnificence and their own excesses, and inevitably fell from the sky. It's been happening for thousands of years and will happen again. Others, on the ground grieve and guilt, having done what they could. Others are shocked in their innocence, blind to the pattern. But sometimes, all we can do is watch the tragedy unfold.

Bibliography

Bly, Robert (2004) *Iron John: A Book About Men.* Da Capo Press.
De la Bère, Rupert (1938) *Icarus: An Anthology of the Poetry of Flight.* London: Macmillan.
Hillman, James (1979) *Puer Papers.* Spring Publications.
Jung, C G *Collected Works.* Princeton University Press.
Owen, Michael (2002) *Jung and the Native American Moon Cycles: Rhythms of Influence.* Nicolas-Hays.
_____ (2012)*The Maya Book of Life: Understanding the Xultun Tarot.* Kahurangi Press.
_____ (2018) *All the Rough Beasts: The Death of the Earth, Part 1.* Kahurangi Press.
Porterfield, Sally et al (2009) *Perpetual adolescence: Jungian analyses of American media, literature, and pop culture.* SUNY Press.
von Franz, Marie-Louise (2000) *The Problem of the Puer Aeternus.* 3rd ed. Inner City Books.

Index

MORE FROM KAHURANGI PRESS

www.kahurangi-press.com
www.deathoftheearth.com
www.xultun.com

by Michael Owen

All the Rough Beasts: The Death of the Earth, Part 1

The Maya Book of Life: Understanding the Xultun Tarot

Jung and the Native American Moon Cycles

by Peter Balin

Xultun Tarot (Classic Edition)

All titles available from Amazon

www.ingramcontent.com/pod-product-compliance
Lightning Source LLC
Chambersburg PA
CBHW060502280326
41933CB00014B/2827